The Leadership Compass:
Values and Ethics in Higher Education

by John R. Wilcox and Susan L. Ebbs

ASHE-ERIC Higher Education Report No. 1, 1992

Prepared by

Clearinghouse on Higher Education
The George Washington University

In cooperation with

Association for the Study
of Higher Education

Published by

School of Education and Human Development
The George Washington University

Jonathan D. Fife, Series Editor

Cite as
Wilcox, John R., and Susan L. Ebbs. 1992. *The Leadership Compass: Values and Ethics in Higher Education.* ASHE-ERIC Higher Education Report No. 1. Washington, D.C.: The George Washington University, School of Education and Human Development.

Library of Congress Catalog Card Number 92-85441
ISSN 0884-0040
ISBN 1-878380-14-1

Managing Editor: Bryan Hollister
Manuscript Editor: Barbara Fishel, Editech
Cover design by Michael David Brown, Rockville, Maryland

The ERIC Clearinghouse on Higher Education invites individuals to submit proposals for writing monographs for the *ASHE-ERIC Higher Education Report* series. Proposals must include:
1. A detailed manuscript proposal of not more than five pages.
2. A chapter-by-chapter outline.
3. A 75-word summary to be used by several review committees for the initial screening and rating of each proposal.
4. A vita and a writing sample.

ERIC Clearinghouse on Higher Education
School of Education and Human Development
The George Washington University
One Dupont Circle, Suite 630
Washington, DC 20036-1183

This publication was prepared partially with funding from the Office of Educational Research and Improvement, U.S. Department of Education, under contract no. ED RI-88-062014. The opinions expressed in this report do not necessarily reflect the positions or policies of OERI or the Department.

EXECUTIVE SUMMARY

What Is the Impetus for Assessing the Values and Ethics of Higher Education?

Colleges and universities are custodians of knowledge. Because the possession of knowledge is the source of *power,* understood here as the ability to influence decisions in contemporary society, these institutions are also the gateway to power, significantly affecting the quality of economic and social life throughout the world. Thus, insofar as colleges and universities create and disseminate knowledge within a particular society, they are institutions with *moral* responsibilities to maintain the well-being of that society.

Why Is the Collegiate Ethos So Important to Values And Ethics in Higher Education?

The role of the higher education professional should be looked at by means of ethical analysis more broadly conceived than scrutinizing campus ethical dilemmas under the microscope of ethical theories. Of cardinal importance is the impact of *ethos*—customs, practices, and institutional contexts—on the quality of life and on the ability to sustain a connected view of things characterized by loyalty, commitment, and love (Kuh and Whitt 1988; Palmer 1987). With a focus on the ethos of higher education, any normative discussion of ethics— and of values—takes place within the broader contexts of organizational structure and society.

What Is an Ethics of the Ethos?

Morality is not an issue only when problems arise. Responsibility for individual and social welfare is part of the institutional landscape, a daily occurrence manifested in decision making on all levels of the college or university and in the goals toward which the decision making is directed. An ethical analysis that highlights the interconnectedness of all elements in the institution—an ethics of ethos—brings to attention the complexity of the moral life and the subtle nature of responsibility in higher education.

What Dimensions of Higher Education Merit Attention?
The professoriat

Work in academic life, like any other kind of work, is laden with values and has a moral dimension that emerges from the ethical reflection characteristic of institutional self-scrutiny.

Work contributes to personal identity, has a social meaning, and is best understood as a vocation or calling. The scholar has considerable power "to define reality" for and exercise control over society in general and students in particular. Students are vulnerable before and unequal to the scholar; trust must characterize faculty-student relationships. Ultimately, however, professorial knowledge is not proprietary but communal, dedicated to the welfare of society through the transmission and extension of knowledge. The role of the scholar can be conceived in four phases: teaching, discovery, application, and integration, each of which has its own ethical assumptions and problems (Boyer 1990). Often the competing needs of these roles cause conflicts for the scholar teacher/researcher. In responding to these problems, the scholar must balance individual with group realities and requirements. An important pedagogical conception to help achieve the balance is the learning community.

Leadership

Leadership in higher education continues to be under intense pressure to respond to societal issues resulting from trends in demographics and enrollment and economic and social forces that bring both possible disruption and/or opportunity. The use of values expressed by the mission statement and ethical reflection as resources in decision making can positively affect the institution's ability to respond to complex decisions about funding and the budget.

The institution's primary leadership role, attributed to the president with ethical as well as academic responsibility, is complicated by the expectation of shared governance with faculty. Success in shared governance requires the ability to use more than one organizational model to respond to situations and multiple realities (Bensimon, Neumann, and Birnbaum 1989). Practices of leadership that focus on collaborative efforts to encourage dialogue, emphasize the shared values of the mission statement, and create an atmosphere of trust all contribute to integrative processes and solutions (Fisher and Tack 1988). Strategic planning provides a structured opportunity for faculty, administrators, staff, and students to work collaboratively and constructively with values necessary for institutional effectiveness and overall integrity.

Models of ethical decision making help inform the practice of successful leadership in the face of ever-increasing complexities in higher education. These models have in common the process of defining the issues, making decisions by reviewing alternatives based on intuitive evaluation or on ethical rules and principles, deciding whether to carry out the action, and then implementing it using the best deliberative judgment.

Student life

Students on today's campuses encounter a variety of complex situations for which they are often ill-prepared by experience or individual development. The relationship between students' attitudes and values and the environment that supports or challenges them stands as a dynamic dialectic of confirmation and rejection that affects the ethical positions and choices of both the individual and the institution. The distinctive nature of the institutional ethos affects the values and *culture* interests manifested in the campus climate and the overall effect of the college experience on the student.

Theoretical models for understanding students' development help to provide faculty and administrators with data to enhance students' learning by responding effectively to students' increasingly diverse needs. Research in the areas of gender, cultural, and ethnic differences in cognitive and psychosocial development over the past 10 years has ethical implications for college teaching, educational policies, and student affairs programs and services.

Issues facing higher education, such as racism, sexism, homophobia, substance abuse, and academic dishonesty, argue for the pursuit of an ethical environment that consistently asserts the importance of human dignity, nourishes growth and achievement, and insists on respect in interpersonal communication and relations.

What Direction Does an Ethics of the Ethos Provide?

The literature detailing the immorality of individual actions or policies underscores a more pervasive problem in higher education: the lack of community and the lack of a sense of shared values that give direction and purpose (Bellah et al. 1985, 1991). Strategic planning for the future must emphasize the learning community as the institutionalization of a program that responds to concern for values and ethics in higher education (Gabelnick et al. 1990).

What Is the Learning Community?

The learning community can be provisionally construed as an ideal type of higher education culture that seeks to overcome current tendencies toward individual alienation and intellectual fragmentation with regard to present academic specialization and special interests. The learning community does not deny the value of research or the scholar's freedom of inquiry, but, as a moral community, it does seek to organize them within an ethical domain of connectedness and mutual responsibility.

Why Is the Learning Community So Important?

The learning community embraces a distinctive ethos, one that is laden with values and sustains the only fitting context for ethical analysis. Based on the curriculum, the learning community addresses many important concerns already touched on. The learning community enables faculty who feel isolated by the limits of their discipline and miss the richness they knew so well in graduate school to reach out to other disciplines. At the same time, learning communities address the growing diversity among students in terms of age, race, ethnicity, religion, and marital and enrollment status. Most important, the learning community allows for a wide variety of applications, not simply application in the small liberal arts college.

How Can Colleges and Universities Develop Learning Communities?

One effective way to develop a learning community is the values audit. This campuswide process is a means of assessing the discrepancy between explicit and implicit values and the decisions that flow from them (Wilcox and Ebbs 1992). It is an effective tool for bringing the administration, faculty, staff, and students together. The values audit is not an end in itself, however: It is only a powerful catalytic agent in the creation of learning communities. Learning communities require commitment and continual nourishment by all sectors of the institution.

—O—

In many ways, the learning community brings together the themes of leadership, faculty, and students. Leadership is essential to colleges' and universities' sensitivity to values in higher education. The learning community symbolizes the delicate nature of that task. At the same time, collaboration among faculty in this learning project is of the essence. Such communities can bring out the best in faculty and resolve several of the tensions faculty face in their careers, especially the tension between research and teaching. Community gives direction to students and anchors their collegiate experience in the intellectual life (Astin 1985). Only such an approach will do justice to the complexity of ethical issues facing higher education.

ADVISORY BOARD

Alberto F. Cabrera
State University of New York–Albany

Jay L. Chronister
University of Virginia

Carol Everly Floyd
Board of Regents of the Regency Universities System
State of Illinois

Elizabeth Hawthorne
University of Toledo

L. Jackson Newell
University of Utah

Barbara Taylor
Association of Governing Boards of Universities and Colleges

CONSULTING EDITORS

A. Nancy Avakian
Metropolitan State University

Paula Y. Bagasao
University of California System

Margaret J. Barr
Texas Christian University

Rose R. Bell
New School for Social Research

David G. Brown
University of North Carolina–Asheville

Jay L. Chronister
University of Virginia

Clifton F. Conrad
University of Wisconsin–Madison

James Cooper
FIPSE College Teaching Project

Richard A. Couto
Tennessee State University

John W. Creswell
University of Nebraska–Lincoln

Donald F. Dansereau
Texas Christian University

Virginia N. Gordon
Ohio State University

Wesley R. Habley
American College Testing

Michael L. Hanes
West Chester University

Dianne Horgan
Memphis State University

Joan Isenberg
George Mason University

Susan Jeffords
University of Washington

Greg Johnson
Harvard College

Margaret C. King
Schenectady County Community College

Donald Kirby
Le Moyne College

Joseph Lowman
University of North Carolina

Jean MacGregor
Evergreen State College

Christine Maitland
National Education Association

Richard L. Morrill
University of Richmond

R. Eugene Rice
Antioch University

C. Arthur Sandeen
University of Florida

David C. Smith
North Central College

Carol F. Stoel
American Association for Higher Education

Susan Stroud
Brown University

Stuart Suss
City University of New York–Kingsborough

Marilla D. Svinicki
University of Texas–Austin

Elizabeth Watson
California State University–Humboldt

Janice Weinman
The College Board

Roger B. Winston
University of Georgia

REVIEW PANEL

Charles Adams
University of Massachusetts–Amherst

Louis Albert
American Association for Higher Education

Richard Alfred
University of Michigan

Philip G. Altbach
State University of New York–Buffalo

Marilyn J. Amey
University of Kansas

Louis C. Attinasi, Jr.
University of Houston

Robert J. Barak
Iowa State Board of Regents

Alan Bayer
Virginia Polytechnic Institute and State University

John P. Bean
Indiana University

Louis W. Bender
Florida State University

John M. Braxton
Syracuse University

Peter McE. Buchanan
Council for Advancement and
    Support of Education

John A. Centra
Syracuse University

Arthur W. Chickering
George Mason University

Shirley M. Clark
Oregon State System of Higher Education

Darrel A. Clowes
Virginia Polytechnic Institute and State University

John W. Creswell
University of Nebraska–Lincoln

Deborah DiCroce
Piedmont Virginia Community College

Richard Duran
University of California

Kenneth C. Green
University of Southern California

Edward R. Hines
Illinois State University

Marsha W. Krotseng
West Virginia State College and University Systems

George D. Kuh
Indiana University–Bloomington

Daniel T. Layzell
Arizona Legislature

Meredith Ludwig
American Association of State Colleges and Universities

Mantha V. Mehallis
Florida Atlantic University

Robert J. Menges
Northwestern University

Toby Milton
Essex Community College

James R. Mingle
State Higher Education Executive Officers

Gary Rhoades
University of Arizona

G. Jeremiah Ryan
Harford Community College

Daryl G. Smith
Claremont Graduate School

William Tierney
Pennsylvania State University

Susan Twombly
University of Kansas

Harold Wechsler
University of Rochester

Michael J. Worth
George Washington University

CONTENTS

FOREWORD

Higher education is an organization that society has given a great deal of respect and freedom. One example of this respect is that it is one of the few professional entities that is self-regulated and has no external certification for its professional staff. This distinctive position originally was the result of four factors. First, a college education was considered important primarily to the intellectually and socially elite. Second, the intellectual activities of colleges were mysterious and felt to be beyond the understanding of the average person. Third, while it was fashionable for a community to have a college, its size and demand on the public dollar were small. Fourth, and most important, colleges, along with the church, were considered the moral leaders of society.

While all four factors contributed to society's willingness to grant higher education a privileged status, it was the high moral and ethical standards that colleges constantly espoused that gave higher education its position of leadership. People were confident that colleges did not need regulation because they had an unquestionable moral compass for guidance.

Over the years, higher education's role of leadership has changed considerably. Higher education is now considered one of the most important social institutions in our society for many good reasons. It has helped lead the world in research, as evidenced by the number of its Nobel laureates; almost all professions require some form of higher education for certification; and, as indicated by employment statistics, a college education is almost mandatory to get and keep a high-paying job. What also has changed is society's faith in the values and ethics that make up higher education's leadership compass.

When an organization believes that it is too complex to be able to clearly articulate its mission; when as one of its fundamental values it believes that it does not deal with customers; and when it continues to hold a major portion of its professional staff—the tenured faculty—unaccountable for their effectiveness, something must be available that the public can point to to maintain its faith in the enterprise. As long as higher education could point to the values and ethics that it used to guide its actions and demonstrate that faculty and graduates represented these values, society remained content. Twenty years ago, however, with Watergate demonstrating the questionable values of the college-trained professionals involved, the public's faith in the values and ethics of higher education was severely shaken. Subsequent events, including higher education's reluctance to lead in such social areas as equality in race and gender, age discrimination, and access for the disabled, and the misuse of public indirect cost funding for research projects, continue to undermine the public's trust.

The consideration of values and ethics is of prime importance to the future of higher education. John R. Wilcox, director of the Center for Professional Ethics at Manhattan College, and Susan L. Ebbs, associate vice president and dean of student life at St. John's University, have undertaken this review of the ethical issues that higher education needs to address in the 1990s. They examine these issues by looking at leadership, scholarship, and students' development and conclude with the importance that values and ethics have for the future of the learning community.

In higher education, at least three conditions are necessary to ensure the congruency of values and ethics. First is a willingness to consciously identify those values and ethics that are essential to the academy. Second is the development of a consistent process of evaluation that will assess the degree to which these values and ethics are represented in the actions of the members of the academy. And third is the assurance that a reward system is in operation to clearly reflect the pleasure or displeasure of the organization when these values and ethics are or are not present. This report is the start of that process.

Jonathan D. Fife
Series Editor
Professor of Higher Education Administration and
Director, ERIC Clearinghouse on Higher Education

PREFACE

Colleges and universities are custodians of knowledge. The possession of knowledge is the source of *power,* understood in this monograph as the ability to influence decisions in contemporary society. As a result, these institutions are also the gateway to power, having significant effects on the quality of economic and social life throughout the world. Thus, insofar as colleges and universities create and disseminate knowledge within a particular society, they are institutions with *moral* responsibilities to maintain the well-being of that society.

In addition to discovering and imparting knowledge, colleges and universities offer to society some of the most formidable criticism of these learning processes. U.S. institutions of higher learning have a tradition of self-scrutiny and evaluation that deeply affects the ethical evaluations of this country's higher education. As the distribution of knowledge—and power—becomes more diffuse in relation to new multicultural realities in our society at large, these institutions work harder than ever to understand their increasingly complex role in addressing issues and making choices that support democratic rights and assumptions, fundamental values upon which U.S. education is built. The values and ethics inherent in U.S. higher education are as diverse as the backgrounds and experiences of its various student, professorial, and administrative constituents. This report organizes and critiques this wide-ranging discourse, examining ethical questions that range from issues involving corruption in athletic programs to the competing values inherent in the professoriat's dual role of scholar and teacher.

The introduction addresses the need for institutional self-scrutiny. In addition to surveying the literature that pertains to such self-analysis, it also presents the operative ethical terms and concepts with which the entire report is concerned. It offers an "ethics of ethos," a concept that will be refined, in subsequent sections, in terms of the "learning community." The broad dimensions of this ethical analysis are elaborated in sections on leadership, the professoriat, and campus culture (focusing primarily on student life). From a variety of contexts, the report revisits such ethical problems as defining and assessing academic integrity, freedom of speech, and the conflicts between the rights of the individual and the needs of the academic community. It pays particular attention to the ethical problems posed by new and changing multicultural student populations. The goal toward which the report and analysis move is the creation of a learning community (Boyer 1990; Gabelnick et al. 1990), the principal subject of the final section. The concluding section also considers the means by which the learning community is developed; chief among them is the *values audit* (Reynolds and Smith 1990; Smith 1984; Smith and Reynolds 1990).

This report, rather than being a survey of ethics courses or curricula, is a review of ethical issues many of the participants in higher education face in the 1990s. Its intention is to aid faculty and administrators in their often daunting need to keep abreast of current ethical concerns by providing a comprehensive bibliographic review of the relevant literature and a thematic organization of it, thereby providing an effective framework for analysis. In sum, this report is a means of stimulating the moral imagination of faculty and administrators as they assess the increasing number of divergent and highly visible moral problems on our campuses.

INTRODUCTION

Let us note that moral education takes place least in class-room lectures (although [they] have a place) and is only in a limited measure a matter of developing moral rea-soning. To a much greater extent, moral education is fostered through personal example and above all through fostering the proper institutional culture—from corridors and cafeteria to the parking lot and sports. In effect, the whole school should be considered as a set of experiences generating situations where young people either learn the values of civility, sharing, and responsibility to the common good or of cheating, cut-throat competition, and total self-absorption ("The Responsive Communitarian Platform" 1991–92, p. 10).

Institutional Self-Scrutiny: Needs and Forms

Higher education has its share of moral problems that prompt ethical analysis. Athletic scandals, discriminatory admissions policies, and sexual violence immediately come to mind, but on a more fundamental level are, in the minds of many within the academy and in our society generally, a crisis of values on the campus and a consequent confusion about the mission of higher education. This confusion is evident from several questions: What is the purpose of the core curriculum, and what should students learn about nonwestern cultures? What is the aim of a liberal education, and how is the development of individual students related to the well-being of society? Because contemporary higher education is a corporate enterprise, how does this status relate to the demands of students for a more personalized education?

In view of these issues, self-scrutiny becomes a moral imperative for institutions of higher learning.

In view of these issues, self-scrutiny becomes a moral imperative for institutions of higher learning. That is, institutions have an obligation in conscience to be self-reflective regarding their various powers and responsibilities. The undeniability of these obligations is reinforced by governmental requirements for institutional self-assessment to ensure economic cost-effectiveness (Caplan 1980). Little doubt exists that "institutional self-assessment provides the threshold for moral consciousness in the college or university" (Lenn and Lenn 1990, p. 348), and colleges and universities already engage in self-examination in a number of ways. For example, funding agencies require outcome assessments, or formal evaluations of the success of students' learning. Accrediting agencies require self-studies on regular cycles, state education

departments require five-year plans, and individual departments sponsor their own self-evaluations. More frequently
in recent years, outcome assessments have been mandated
as a form of self-analysis. Eighty-two percent of all colleges
now report such assessments under way (El-Khawas 1990);
such activities had increased from 55 percent in 1988 to 67
percent in 1989. A direct connection seems to exist between
assessment procedures and the institutional mission, the
objectives of which are articulated in a mission statement.
Likewise, scholars agree that such procedures require the
acceptance of certain values, one of them that faculty and
institutions share with the student the responsibility for learning. Most recognize that effective outcome assessments
require a previous investigation of the values that inform the
institutional mission and the decision making of all constituents (Kean 1987).

Institutional Self-Assessment and the Articulation of Values

Assessments of students' learning, the self-study and program
evaluation among them, require that institutions measure
progress against some commonly held benchmark, most often
an articulated mission or value system. The primary form of
assessment is "self-evaluation that is oriented toward renewing
a clear sense of purpose" (Lenn and Lenn 1990, p. 342). Self-
assessment also requires building a moral dimension into
communities so that well-being and social responsibility are
both increased. A practical way to build in the moral dimension is through the use of a values audit. This instrument
assists the campus community in understanding divergences
between the stated mission and goals of the institution and
the community's perception of how the actual practices of
administrators, faculty, staff, and students diverge from the
college's or university's documents. The processes of com-
pleting the audit and carrying out recommendations are of
great value. They both take priority over any written report.
Important as it is, the values audit is a catalyst and a first step
in enhancing the life of the learning community. It is not a
substitute for that life.

Regardless of the form that a particular institution's assessment of values takes, the outcome should increase sensitivity
toward consensus building and the processes of setting values
(Pace 1979; Reynolds and Smith n.d., 1990; Smith n.d., 1984;

Smith and Reynolds 1990; Wilcox and Ebbs 1992). Although a principal objective of this report is to present a survey of the literature on ethics in higher education, a second goal is to relate this survey to certain key concepts and activities involving the moral dimension of self-assessment. Certainly, these concepts and activities reflect the authors' concerns and biases, but their thematic and organizational preferences neither limit unfairly the survey of literature nor stifle competing ideas or issues.

At first glance, many of the citations in the list of references might not appear to directly address ethical issues. When one recalls the essentially interdisciplinary nature of applied ethics and the nature of higher education as a complex institution having individual and societal goals, however, the bibliographical diversity and scope become intelligible and needed. Problematic areas related to the professoriat, leadership, and campus life are not discrete concerns but interrelated issues, because they are all aspects of the learning community, a term associated with the pioneering work of Patrick Hill and his associates (Gabelnick et al. 1990). This report closely ties ethical discourse to an analysis of the values that are the foundation of higher education but do not lend themselves to the analytic precision so often associated with ethical critique.

An Ethics of Ethos
Thus, it is therefore not the purpose of this report to scrutinize campus ethical dilemmas under the microscope of ethical theories like utilitarianism and deontology. Rather, the approach is to look at the role of the professional in higher education by means of ethical analysis more broadly conceived. Of cardinal importance is the impact of *ethos*—customs, practices, and institutional contexts—on the quality of life and on the ability to sustain a connected view of things characterized by loyalty, commitment, and love (Kuh and Whitt 1988). "A reflective focus upon ethos is more likely to develop in the direction of an understanding and criticism of the institutions of professional life, including professional organizations, education, and the settings within which professionals practice" (Sullivan 1990, p. 191; see also Gustafson 1991). By focusing attention on the ethos of higher education, any normative discussion of ethics thus takes place within the broader contexts of organizational structure and society.

Values, the moral life, and ethics are part of the perennial
need for self-examination and renewal and are relevant for
the diverse set of institutions that come under the umbrella
of higher education in the United States. Distinctiveness
requires continual reinforcement of those qualities defining an institution. All colleges and universities have a responsibility to be faithful to their legal and moral charters,
charters making them accountable to some higher authority:
the state or local government or an ethnic, racial, or religious community.

We have undertaken this project because we believe that
colleges and universities are moral agents. Higher education
assumes social responsibilities toward students by taking on
the task of enhancing their ability to learn in the classroom
and through cocurricular life on campus, a recurring theme
in subsequent sections. Education also acknowledges a
responsibility toward society, because learning helps meet
not only individual needs but also those of the community.
Social responsibility is further fulfilled through the expansion
of the knowledge base by means of research and technological development. Thus, the ethics of ethos in the world of
higher education seeks to forge connections among the often
competing needs of the individual and society, the expansion
of knowledge, and the advancement of technology. The
authors' assumption is that the purposes of individuals and
agencies alike are better served and more morally secure
when they operate within a "community" that values feelings
of connectedness, mutual responsibility, and the fair and balanced exercise of power.

Higher education by its nature is a moral endeavor that
advocates certain highly prized activities or patterns of behavior. These activities or patterns—individual learning and
research—represent values. They are also means for reaching
other values like personal growth and the common good.
Achievement of personal and social values requires other
value-laden means that further confirm the moral agency of
academics and academe. Among these means are respect for
the dignity of the person as an individual and as a member
of diverse groups, academic freedom, and a well-thought-
out pedagogy.

As is already evident, "ethics" is an important term in this
report, requiring definition. As used in this report, it means
the normative analysis of the moral agency of individuals and

institutions and the values they seek. While principles of consequences and obligation (to name but two normative means of understanding and codifying values) give direction to decision making and shed light on the value of values, the moral agency of colleges and universities remains comprehensive. Morality is not an issue only when problems arise. Responsibility for individual and social welfare is part of the institutional landscape, a daily occurrence manifested in decision making on all levels of the college or university and in the goals toward which the decision making is directed. An ethical analysis that highlights the interconnectedness of all elements in the institution—an ethics of the ethos—brings to attention the complexity of the moral life and the subtle nature of responsibility in higher education.

In light of these assumptions, three dimensions of higher education merit particular attention in this report: the professoriat (the following section), leadership (the second section), and campus culture, focusing primarily on student life (the third section). A review of the literature in these areas reveals a host of ethical problems, from athletic scandals to faculty plagiarism. Ethical categories, such as equity, fairness, and honesty, easily lead to moral judgments on these problems. At the same time, however, it becomes obvious that the literature detailing the immorality of individual actions or policies underscores a more pervasive problem in higher education: the lack of community and the lack of a sense of shared values that give direction and purpose. The authors' recommendations for future directions place great emphasis on community and the concept of the learning community as the institutionalization of a program that responds to the concerns raised in the other sections. Although the final section explores the concept of the learning community more fully, a brief definition here will enable the reader to compare and evaluate ideas presented in the earlier sections.

The *learning community* can be provisionally construed as an ideal type of higher education culture that seeks to overcome current tendencies toward individual alienation and intellectual fragmentation with regard to present academic specialization and special interests. It is a response to the complexity and diversity of university and college departmentalization and to the destabilizing aspects of the proliferation of knowledge characteristic of contemporary research enterprises. The learning community does not deny the value of research or the scholar's freedom of enquiry, but, as a moral community, it does seek to organize them within an ethical domain of connectedness and mutual responsibility.

While a review of the history of higher education in the United States would provide a context for the present discussion, such a review is beyond the purposes of this report. The reader should note, however, that concern for values and ethics is not a new issue on our campuses. From the earliest days of higher education in this country, colleges and universities have been part of the nation-building process (Kimball 1986; see also Cremin 1980; Potts 1981; Sloan 1980). Historically, colleges functioned as moral enterprises (Bok 1990), in contrast to the way some think of higher education today: self-serving institutions that motivate students to seek personal interests and careers (DePalma 1991a; Laney 1990). A harbinger of the present interest in the moral life of colleges and universities is found in, among others, *The Higher Learning in America* (Hutchins 1936), an attempt to introduce coherence and a clear vision of undergraduate education. The writings of Ernest Boyer, Derek Bok, and A. Bartlett Giamatti have carried that tradition into the present.

This discussion of ethics in higher education is by no means intended as an analysis of existing ethics curricula. This report is not interested in what is taught in philosophy class; instead, the authors are concerned about directing ethical analysis toward the various types of academic communities themselves. They intend to articulate an ethos of higher education that assesses the life and well-being of academia and to recommend various means of redressing the institutional failings that have been discovered in that environment.

*The hope for flexibility and openness to rational moral per-
suasion is the hope that for the healthy and well-integrated
personality, the Aristotelian ideal, the role of the good person,
will at least limit all other roles the person may play* (Goldman 1980, p. 292).

The Meanings of "Profession"

The word "profession" has religious origins. "To profess" has
a clear resonance within the Roman Catholic monastic tradition wherein members of religious orders profess vows publicly. They affirm membership in a community and proclaim
a willingness to fulfill the mission of the group as set forth
by the rules of the order. Neither expertise nor service are
in the historic roots of the term (Schurr 1982). Originally,
being a professional meant vowing to uphold commitment
to poverty, chastity, and obedience in a community. A "transcendent intent" was and is (now redefined to account for
the obligations of contemporary professionalism) intrinsic
to this commitment.

We live, however, in an age suspicious of transcendent
claims. Ideals like "the glory of truth," so common in the history of education today, often seem impossible to sustain.
Indeed, the goals of the academic community—just like those
of U.S. society at large—often seem ill formed or conflicting.
Certainly, then, those who "profess" to knowledge in today's
colleges and universities must continually reflect on the relationship between personal interests (based on one's own
knowledge) and those of the community. Standards against
which this relationship might be measured and appraised are
neither clear nor universal. A core of professional standards
and codes of ethics, however, express and advance certain
generally accepted ethical norms. These standards and codes
can be used to help orient ethical inquiry into more equiv-
ocal matters.

Professional Standards and Codes of Ethics

Ordinarily, associations made up of professionals set their
own standards to ensure the competence and integrity of
members engaged in private practice and to monitor their
conduct. In many cases, professional standards are reinforced
by civil law through a process of examinations and licensing.
Medicine, law, and divinity are considered the classic pro-

---

fessions. Because college and university education is required for certification in these professions and because the educators are defined by characteristics similar to these other groups, higher education can also be considered a profession (Wilcox 1989). Education is one of the three secular professions attached to or derived from the clerical state or religious profession (Camenisch 1983). The concern is not so much with the religious origins as with the exceptional commitment involved—an atypical moral undertaking not expected of all. Attention is more easily given to law and medicine because of the level of power wielded by lawyers and doctors as opposed to teachers and clerics (Camenisch 1983).

Higher education has formal codes and policy statements that address faculty behavior. Nevertheless, no "definitive organized association that upholds membership requirements and maintains ethical norms" exists (Schurr 1982, p. 318). The code crafted by the American Association of University Professors (AAUP) comes closest perhaps to the maintenance of such norms. An explanation of the meaning and purpose of codes is helpful here, however, to elucidate an evaluation of the AAUP code and of codes for the professoriat more generally. Codes or statements of ethics seem to be necessary when a cohesive culture no longer exists (Reynolds and Smith 1990). The growing presence of codes, for the academic community of administrators and professors as well as classic and aspiring professions, underlines the absence of consensus on deep values in the society (Bellah et al. 1985; Sullivan 1990). Given the public demand for legislation in a growing number of states covering effective instruction and responsible evaluation as well as the general erosion of consensus over values within society and the academic community, however, mandated codes of professional conduct could well be forthcoming.

The AAUP promulgated its initial code of conduct on professional ethics for the professoriat in 1966 (American Association 1987), although the AAUP's Committee B on Professional Ethics was formed in the early 1920s (Dill 1982a). John Dewey chaired this committee, which, after a few meetings, remained dormant until 1956, when a short statement was submitted to the AAUP Council, which then rejected it. In 1966, the "Statement on Professional Ethics" was finally adopted and then revised in 1987 with sections on inclusive language and references to harassment and discrimination.

In five brief sections, the statement discusses the values that should guide professional life: growth in scholarly competence, students' learning, and responsibility to colleagues, institution, and society. The statement also presents specific activities to be avoided, among them conflicts of interest, exploitation of students, and harassment of colleagues. Despite this stated commitment to ethical behavior, AAUP has always made clear that its primary concern is academic freedom and tenure (1984; Rich 1984). By doing so, AAUP protects its constituents. By investigating charges about ethics, AAUP appears to assist the administration. It is in the best interest of the professoriat to expose unethical professors, however (Rich 1984). Further, the AAUP Statement is too short, leaves important concerns, such as outside employment, to other documents, and makes no provision for implementation (Rich 1984).

The growing presence of codes . . . underlines the absence of consensus on deep values in the society.

The multiple moral issues on campus reflect the rapidly changing society in which higher education in the United States exists. Scholars disagree, however, regarding the usefulness of an academic code of ethics, one that would govern the work of professors. Some reject academic codes as both ineffective and difficult to construct (Callahan 1982; Schurr 1982). A code is "antithetical to the ethical foundation of the academic profession" (Schurr 1982). Another scholar, however, affirms the usefulness of codes to provide a process of self-scrutiny that would be constructive. Among the issues needing attention are general offenses like sexual harassment and discrimination as well as problem areas in teaching and research that involve specialized responsibilities (Nickel 1990).

An ongoing institutional examination of conscience on the subject of academic ethics, a *valuing process,* has been proposed as the only viable solution (Callahan 1982). Indeed, some institutionalized process seems to be the only effective means of coping with institutional complexity, the range of moral issues facing faculty, and the changing expectations of the larger society.

The responsibility for moral self-scrutiny has been placed at both the institutional and personal levels, calling for systemic and personal professional scrutiny (Reynolds and Smith 1990). These academic principles of responsibility are based on identified deep values: respect for people, honesty in all communications, virtues of fairness and efficiency, and commitment to the common good. Although these values could be in competition in specific instances (for example, respect for people versus the need for efficiency), in principle they are mutually supportive and consistent (Reynolds and Smith 1990).

Central to the discussion of the ethics of any professional field is the extent to which the special norms and principles governing the professions override individual rights and other moral principles. Clearly, it varies with the profession and with the instance (Goldman 1980; Rich 1984). Is scientific research with dangerous technological or social consequences permissible? (Goldman 1980). Adherence to or denial of special norms as a result of academic role differentiation is important in such a case. "Can professional, in this case academic, license or duty to seek and report the truth in such areas [nuclear physics, sociological investigations of racial intelligence] override the potential social harm from the findings no matter how disastrous?" (Goldman 1980, p. 287; see also Passmore 1984).

Following this line of reasoning, one might ask other questions about academic role differentiation. Do the principles of tenure and academic freedom weaken the responsibilities of teaching students and presenting controversial issues with objectivity? (Passmore 1984). Does the academic reward system based on publication diminish excellence in teaching and service to the college or the local and national communities? The problem is not so much living up to ethical standards in professional life, but rather assuming without question that they ought to be lived (Goldman 1980).

In themselves, the norms of professional ethics do not define the social or personal relationships of individuals toward one another. These norms focus on obligations arising out of contractual agreements. This issue is important for educators whose relationship with students and the college or university community encompasses far more than contractual agreements (Reynolds and Smith 1990). While higher education has become a highly rationalized institution with characteristics of contract, bureaucracy, and impersonality *(gesellschaft),* it has other characteristics—openness, trust, commitment, care, concern for meaning, transcendence and ultimacy—more frequently associated with community *(gemeinschaft)* (see Tonnies 1963 for a discussion of the ideal types represented here). These communitarian characteristics are at the core of professorial identity.

The Roles of the Modern Scholar

The literature dealing with the professoriat is as extensive and varied as the multifaceted roles assigned to it (Finkelstein 1987). Generally speaking, *roles* can be understood as practices or coherent patterns of individual activity that produce goods internal to the activity. Professors assume a variety of roles to realize a variety of goals, each of which maintains a constellation of related moral imperatives. Boyer identifies four functions that constitute the professor's scholarly and professional identity: *discovery, integration, application,* and *teaching* (Boyer 1990; Sullivan 1990). These functions stand as the basis of a particular professorial role, with scholars frequently assuming more than one (for example, a professor can be both discoverer and teacher) because of individual choice, contractual obligations, or pressures like the reward system. Each role carries certain moral obligations. Moral dilemmas can arise when the goals in each role make demands that compete with each other (Schuster and Bowen 1987).

Boyer's typology

Scholarship Reconsidered (Boyer 1990) presents this four-point typology to describe the role of the scholar. In effect, the typology addresses the question of whether a common profession of teaching exists or whether researchers and members of disciplines are separate (Robertson and Grant 1982). Boyer's proposed solution is to subsume within the role of scholar all the activities of an academic's life—discovery, integration, application, and teaching—acknowledging that conflicts can arise when the requirements to satisfy the goals of one role are incompatible with those needed to satisfy another.

The scholarships of discovery and teaching. The *scholar-discoverer* engages in research leading to new understandings of the natural and social world or reinterpretations of history and literature and theories of pedagogy. These practices produce internal goods that benefit humankind (for example, the discovery of DNA or new theories of linguistics). The realization of these goods also depends on the practice of many virtues but especially justice, courage, and honesty in the work of research.

The practice of the *scholar-teacher* facilitates students' learning, an internal good valuable to the learning community.

Teaching requires the virtues mentioned in the preceding paragraph but also those of patience and understanding, among others. Teaching further demands not only commitment to mastery of the discipline but also excellence in pedagogy to produce those goods internal to the practice.

Certainly the scholarships of discovery and teaching can overlap. Teaching as the transmission, transformation, and extension of knowledge embraces more than mere lecturing. Setting goals, recognizing learning styles in the classroom, and effective assessment are fundamental. Good teaching requires keeping up with developments in the field of expertise. Pedagogy requires planning, ongoing evaluation, the creation of a common ground and learning community characterized by the transformation and extension of knowledge. These descriptions of good teaching fall well within the realm of discovery.

The scholarship of application. Another aspect of the role of the scholar involves his or her commitment to service, defined as the application of knowledge to the resolution of consequential problems within the scholar's discipline, as well as the possible redefinition of the scholarly agenda because of attention to a social problem. "To be considered scholarship, service activities must be tied directly to one's special field of knowledge and relate to, and flow directly out of, this professional activity. Such service is serious, demanding work, requiring the rigor—and the accountability—traditionally associated with research activities" (Boyer 1990, p. 22). This insight is important because of the confusion that has attended the role of service within higher education. Considered committee work or community assistance, service has traditionally been viewed as unrelated to the identity of the scholar, rather than an integral part of it. Seen as applied scholarship, service includes "activities that relate directly to the intellectual work of the professor and carried out through consultation, technical assistance, policy analysis, program evaluation, and the like" (Boyer 1990, p. 36). Service, applied to social or civic projects, is often forgotten in consideration for promotion and tenure. Were there broad acceptance of this notion—of giving faculty credit for service—a number of value conflicts and ethical dilemmas would likely be resolved (Light 1974).

The scholarship of application is a long and important tradition in the humanities (Hastings Center 1984). Professionalization of the humanities at the end of the 19th century is characterized as historically idiosyncratic. The new applied humanities are "a return to the kind of diverse purposes and social roles that have characterized the humanities for most of their history" (p. 12).

The scholarship of integration. Integration is a groundbreaking activity that occurs in different disciplines on the borderlines of discovery (Boyer 1990). It brings together discrete research findings and demonstrates connections among them, thereby demonstrating or suggesting new forms of knowledge. The scholarly role of integration has an influence on the other three roles in that the resulting knowledge could lead to new discovery and application as well as the transformation and extension of knowledge in teaching.

The tension continues between research and teaching and the attendant faculty reward structure (see, e.g., Bok 1990; Rosovsky 1990; Schaefer 1990; Smith 1990). Some are sympathetic to the elite group of researchers on the faculty (Rosovsky 1990) and view performance in research, especially through publication, over teaching ability as the better indicator of success. Others, however, emphasize faculty responsibility in teaching (for example, returning work promptly with adequate comment, giving proper guidance to graduate students writing theses) but do not mention pedagogy itself as a moral responsibility (Bok 1990).

Scholarship versus the academic profession

The role of the scholar can be further complicated by the often competing needs and goals of the scholarly and the academic professions. The term "academic professional" (Dill 1982b) relies on a typology (Light 1974) distinguishing between the faculty and the academic professional. *Faculty* refers to those with academic appointments at colleges and universities, whereas *academic professional scholars* refers to those individuals with academic appointments who are engaged in the advancement of knowledge, train new members of the particular profession, and judge their qualifications. Academic professionals do not consider undergraduate teaching *and* administrative duties as self-identifying

activities; instead these activities are institutional obligations (Light 1974). In addition, a number of academic professionals do no teaching at all; research constitutes their only responsibility. This typology has implications for academic ethics (Dill 1982b). "There is an assumption that the core values of the scholarly profession [those who do research only without academic appointments] are also the appropriate values for socializing the faculty subset" (p. 258).

Because the academic professionals are the "gatekeepers" for admission into the ranks of the faculty in higher education, they emphasize the characteristics of the scholarly profession with which they themselves most identify (Clark 1987a): those of a "free profession" with few if any institutional *or* organizational responsibilities, such as teaching or administration. Those aspiring to faculty rank, therefore, receive little direct preparation for teaching (Clark 1987b), because many consider this role subordinate to the role of research, the latter of which contributes more directly to building the knowledge base of a field. Sabbatical leaves represent institutional support for the faculty's research work, designed as they are to provide time for in-depth research. Similar leaves to assist faculty to improve their teaching skills have never been standard practice in higher education, and the general consensus to date considers that this policy is appropriate.

Some take issue with the theory of the academic disciplines as the dominant force in higher education (Tierney 1988; see also Ruscio 1986). The disciplines interact with both the cultures of the institution and the faculty, and knowledge is a social product with political consequences (Tierney 1988). A conservative Christian college might thus view as divinely given the knowledge or tradition that prescribes the truth of traditional sex roles. The disciplines are understood as sources of these data. At a cutting-edge institution, institutional culture dominates departmental culture. Thus, "institutions in some way play a role in interpreting knowledge. . . . Knowledge is a social construct constantly undergoing interpretation and change on a variety of different levels and in a variety of social contexts" (p. 16). Therefore, any attempt to redefine faculty roles must take into account much more than academic preparation in graduate schools. Institutional culture is a dominant force in the role conflicts that faculty experience. While culture is a theme of the final section of this report, it is important to note here the system of formal advisement, especially in the major, and pervasive informal contact between faculty and students that even the casual visitor observes as a dominant characteristic of higher education in the United States.

Emphasizing institutional culture should not distract us from the issues at hand concerning graduate education. The responsibility of graduate schools to help resolve what some see as the teaching/research dilemma is not clear. Graduate students should learn about the historical background, organizational structure, and culture of higher education and of their discipline (Study Group 1984). Scholars in the field posit that such a background will dispel false expectations about the professoriat and combat disillusionment with the multiple roles and responsibilities that faculty perform. Given the enormous turnover rate in faculty over the next two decades (projections of 563,000 new appointments replacing 663,000 current faculty), especially in the arts and sciences (153,000 new appointments replacing 154,000 at the present time) (Kerr 1991), graduate schools and the academic leadership in higher education have a significant opportunity to examine and restructure graduate education.

Moral Responsibility within Roles

Moral issues can arise when the scholar assumes more than one role. They call for ethical analysis because of the relational nature of morality arising from obligations inherent in every role. Relationships between the discoverer and scientific community and between teacher and student are two important examples. The practices and virtues necessary within a particular role arise from the role itself and flow from the values inherent in that role. For example, extension of the knowledge base requires honesty in research. The following subsection recounts Boyer's typology to identify some of the moral issues and questions that face the scholar, paying particular attention to the problems faced by the scholar-teacher and the scholar-discoverer.

Ethical reflection on the role of scholar-teacher

The moral responsibilities of the scholar-teacher are clear in many instances: Lying to or cruelty toward students should not exist. University teachers also have distinctive responsibilities arising from the conjoining of teaching and research. This moral problem is not easily resolved in view of the mass university and resulting loyalties to a profession. Allegiances to one's discipline are probably more important for faculty than loyalty to the university or even the idea of the university (Shils 1983).

Moral issues also emerge from the modern tendency to divide responsibilities into administration and teaching. Leaving these responsibilities to others, the faculty can weaken the integrity of the college or university whose mission is so closely connected with the work of the faculty (Shils 1983). In other instances, moral problems emerge from the competition between various goods—for example, honesty in grading versus encouragement of the student (Russ 1988). Still others contain no clear institutional guidelines—for example, what are the parameters of students' autonomy in the classroom? Some of these issues have always been present; others reflect the complex nature of contemporary higher education (Robertson and Grant 1982).

Maximum benefit and equal respect. Two ethical principles are almost universally used in assessing moral dilemmas: *maximum benefit* and *equal respect*. Maximizing benefits requires doing what will benefit the greatest number to the greatest extent possible. This principle is balanced by that of equal respect, which views people as ends in themselves: free, rational, and of equal value as moral agents. Both principles are necessary, yet maximum benefit presupposes equal respect. They could, however, conflict. Several germane questions in this regard might be asked: "When is it permissible to violate a person's rights . . . to produce a better outcome?" (Strike 1988, p. 158). When should time be given to weaker students over brighter ones? How much weight, if any, should be given to effort over performance?

The teacher-student relationship has two fundamental moral issues that relate to the principles of maximum benefit and equal respect. The first has to do with understanding students in both formal and informal contacts and contexts, the second with the curriculum. Respect for the "otherness" of students is essential, because an asymmetry of power exists between teachers and students as a result of teachers' expertise, experience, and skills. Respect is expressed in the pedagogical goal of understanding students' grounding: What is their world view and how do they learn?

An issue that has more to do with maximum benefit is the development of a broad-based curriculum. The enhancement of professional ethics programs, for example, is not enough of a response to demands for moral integrity (Buchholz 1989; Hastings Center 1980; Pamental 1988). While educators need to develop and implement effective means of incorporating ethics into the curriculum (Christensen with Hansen 1981; Kuhmerker, Mentkowski, and Erickson 1980), applied and professional ethics are by nature interdisciplinary. Embracing an interdisciplinary approach means abandoning the rigidity and narrowness of departmental structures. It also means forsaking the highly individual approach to teaching that characterizes higher education (Astin 1988; Giroux and Purpel 1983; Hirsch 1988; Schaefer 1990).

Raising these issues highlights other issues: Because the teaching of ethics is itself an ethical issue, whose interests are uppermost when faculty develop curricula? (Meilaender 1989; Waithe and Ozar 1990) and, in a related manner, What value does the college or university professor place on the quality of his or her teaching? Should teaching be considered the primary commitment of the professoriat? While various authors affirm the importance of and obligations in teaching, rarely do they address learning styles and assessment. This formal approach (Cahn 1986; Robinson and Moulton 1985; Rosovsky 1990) stands in sharp contrast to those who emphasize policies, research, and an ethos that brings about increases in students' learning (Boyer 1990; *Policy Perspectives* 1989; Study Group 1984). *Involvement in Learning*, for instance, stresses students' involvement, high expectations, assessment, and feedback as vital to teaching. Each emphasis implies attention to students' needs and is a concrete application of the moral obligation to show respect for students.

While it is a moral imperative for a faculty member to be on time for class, this formal obligation must be grounded in a more comprehensive theory of pedagogy. Reinforcing Boyer's scholarship of teaching is an evaluation of "the commitment of faculty members to teaching through their contributions to the literature on college instruction, student development, and allied topics; to the proceedings of the teaching divisions of learned and professional societies and higher education associations; to instructional materials [like] textbooks and software; and to the development of significant courses and curricula" (Study Group 1984, p. 60). Being on time but then lecturing for 45 minutes falls far short of what is due to students. Publicized office hours that are kept and a presence on campus that cannot be tallied by a precise number of hours also contribute to a comprehensive pedagogy.

Faculty-student collaboration. The traditional student body has changed in terms of ethnic diversity and preparation in skills. Students have become more selective in choosing faculty (Dill 1982b), but these "consumers" of education do not seem to exert any pressure for better teaching. Students' and parents' emphasis remains on institutional prestige, because it is equated with success in one's chosen career or graduate school. The public thus reinforces the emphasis on research, because faculty prestige is highly valued as a sign of institutional fame. It is not only the graduate schools or administrators who are to blame for the lack of emphasis on teaching. Consumers reinforce this type of ethos (Astin 1985; *Policy Perspectives* 1990a). One important force to effect change, however, comes from adult learners, who are fast becoming the majority student group. "These students intuitively ask the right questions: 'Is this course worth the time I spend away from my family and other responsibilities?' 'Should I come again next week or forget it?'" (*Policy Perspectives* 1990a, p. 1; see also *Policy Perspectives* 1990b).

Accountability for students' learning. Insights on the evaluation of students' learning focus on why not much attention has been paid to teaching. Should instructors know what changes are brought about by their teaching? Should they be accountable for students' failure to demonstrate the skills or knowledge for which the course was intended? (Wilson 1982). These somewhat rhetorical questions point to the problem at hand: The professoriat knows very little about effective assessment. And the ethical issue of unsupported claims is involved: "Celebrating reason, demanding demonstration in other realms, we shun assessment, shrug off the notion of accountability, and willingly take credit for the fruits that sun, soil, rain, and Providence have nurtured" (p. 277; see also Stewart 1987).

Lack of rewards. While some evidence suggests that the professoriat increasingly emphasizes teaching (Wycliff 1990), the reward system in institutions of higher education most benefits those engaged in personal development in their respective disciplines. Further, little incentive or movement is apparent toward changing the existing reward structure.

Such change, even if it were warranted, would require strong leadership on all levels of administration, common agreement among peer institutions, and restructuring of graduate education.

The rewards of reputation and promotion or service through lucrative consulting are strong controlling mechanisms. They are goods external to the practice of scholarship and are individual, doing little to promote the common good (MacIntyre 1981). Some scholars decry the rewards of individualism and the battles over requirements for distribution played out by departmental adversaries in full view of the student body. Perhaps most damaging, because it presents a model for work life to the students, is the faculty reward system: "The greatest institutional rewards accrue to those who are most successful in promoting their own professional status and visibility" (Astin 1988, pp. 9–10; see also Carnegie Foundation 1991a, 1991b).

Ethical reflection on the role of scholar-discoverer

More often than not, scholarship in higher education is equated with the function of discovery. While this hallowed role is widely respected within academe and among the public at large, increasing pressures are put on those for whom discovery occupies an important place in their scholarly life to redefine their primary interests. The role has shifted from the scholar pursuing the truth to the professional academic intent on economic support, advancement of a specialized field of knowledge, and satisfaction of interest.

Research versus teaching. A criticism related to the shift from the pursuit of truth to professional advancements is the importance given to research as opposed to teaching (Shapiro 1990). Recently, presidents of leading research universities called for a "new paradigm" in university education to parallel the great changes that took place at the end of the 19th century (Grassmuck 1990). Broad institutional reform and a reassessment of mission are important ways of reducing the pressures associated with the scholarship of discovery. A core issue in the scholarship of scientific discovery is the responsibility to the community for the accuracy of all research (Broad 1991; Hilts 1991a, 1991b; Martin 1989). Knowledge is a communal affair; it is not only a question of personal integrity in the laboratory or being a role model for students.

Broad institutional reform and a reassessment of mission are important ways of reducing the pressures associated with the scholarship of discovery.

The researcher is in solidarity with a much larger community (cf. Niebuhr 1963). Ultimately, the discoverer's responsibility is to the principles of science itself. At the same time, it is important to acknowledge that research is sometimes a solitary activity that occurs as part of a communal project. Solitariness gives added impetus to the need for the virtue of integrity, which leads the discoverer to the practice of honesty when no one is around (Committee on the Conduct 1989; Rich 1984). The communitarian nature of projects can also be an important contributor to virtuous conduct.

Ethics and scientific discovery. The U.S. Congress recently established the Office of Scientific Integrity (OSI) at the National Institutes of Health, charged with the investigation of scientific fraud while avoiding policing. The agency investigates disputed data and acts as arbitrator of facts. Given the thousands of federally sponsored grants and projects, relatively few cases (15) before OSI have resulted in charges of misconduct, a reinforcement of the belief in the scientific community that relatively few instances of fraud, plagiarism, or theft occur (Leary 1991; Wheeler 1991b). While this belief might be true, recent publications dealing with integrity in research indicate great concern for honor in science (Association of American Medical Colleges 1982, 1990; Committee on the Conduct 1989; Institute of Medicine 1989; Sigma Xi 1984). On the heels of the widely publicized fraud case involving Drs. David Baltimore and Thereza Imanishi-Kari, a panel of the National Academy of Sciences has urged the creation of an independent, nonacademic body to develop investigative standards for misconduct, keep track of the misconduct case, and press for ethics education in science (Hilts 1991c).

It is no accident that research claims first attention for many faculty. It yields money, time, travel, visibility, and an esteemed place in the pecking order of published researchers, what has been called "goods external to the practice" (MacIntyre 1981). The quest for these goods further erodes fidelity to the intrinsic qualities of scientific discovery. The financial return on patents resulting from projects could also be a source of considerable conflict between researchers and the administration (Chermside 1985a, 1985b; Crawshaw 1985; Mangan 1987).

Deceptive research: A question of ethics. In the social sciences, belief in the overwhelming need to pursue research could lead to the espousal of a special ethic based on role differentiation that sets the anthropologist or psychologist apart. Leon Festinger's research on cognitive dissonance is a primary example. Did his research group have the right to invade the privacy of those observed and, further, to lie to them for purposes of obtaining their confidence? It is also evident that such "value-free" research presupposes a set of values concerning the importance of social science over against a group's religious or social views and values. A utilitarian calculus that privileges possible benefits over the rights of those studied is the usual ethical criterion by which such research is justified. But some do not believe that such intrusiveness is justified (see, e.g., Bok 1983; Rich 1984; Robinson and Moulton 1985).

Some will claim freedom for scientific inquiry as justification for deceptive research. In research conducted within colleges and universities, this value is reinforced by the canons of academic freedom and tenure and provides potent justification for those engaging in deception. The codes of scientific societies are inadequate, and deceptive research can be challenged on two grounds: the integrity of the research itself and the dignity of those deceived (Bok 1983). Deception can actually skew the study itself—a utilitarian argument—while Kant's categorical imperative supports the right to dignity. Institutionally, the requirement that grant proposals involving humans be approved by an institutional review board puts a brake on deception through procedures requiring informed consent and helps ensure that risks to human subjects in relation to benefits are carefully weighed (Smith 1988). Public debate is now necessary for an issue transcending those that institutional review boards presently face, for example, the transmission of genetic changes through medical therapies (Wheeler 1991a).

Discovery and governmental funding. Closely related to issues of research is the role of the federal government in funding university proposals and contracts. Recent disclosures point to abuses in this area and add to the complex web of ethical issues in higher education. Significant pressure is put on individual faculty members to obtain external funding (Brandt 1987). Explicit or implicit criteria for tenure and promotion, demands for external funding as a source of salary, and competition with other institutions create an environment leading to falsification of data in research findings. The ethos of the college or university itself can obviate the moral freedom of the researcher, who can see no other course of action than fabrication (Streharsky 1988). Given this pressure, it is understandable that federal agencies have also seen the need to develop guidelines to eliminate conflicts of interest on the part of researchers (Wheeler 1989).

A correlative issue is the demand for compensation of overhead written into proposals. While justification exists for reimbursement to the university for laboratory space, computer time, and library resources, the amount of funds sought is difficult to calculate and varies from institution to institution, leaving room for abuse. The use to which these overhead costs is put presents another sensitive moral problem.

Scandals associated with Stanford University's use of overhead funds have prompted federal audits of other research institutions (Celis 1991b). Government and university officials agree, however, that blame is widely shared. Vague federal regulations are liberally interpreted, and government/university audits have been virtually nonexistent (Celis 1991a). The viability of many universities depends on continued funding through federal grants and contracts. This tight fit between government and education symbolizes the educational revolution that began after World War II; it is also symbolic of the responsibility of higher education to the larger society.

Individualism versus the Movement Toward Community

A principal concern of this report is to describe a moral dialectic between the rights and responsibilities of the individual and those of the community of which he or she is part. In some instances, differences between them seem antithetical; in other cases, tensions or apparent contradictions have been resolved. The following discussion recapitulates the dilemma and suggests insights into how the learning community can act to manage it.

Emphasis on individual scholarship

A discussion of the academic profession puts a much-needed emphasis on the institutional context in which the scholar works (Dill 1982b). It is one thing to speak of work as personal calling or vocation, but whether a discernible academic community or just an aggregate of individuals exists is equally important. To what is the institution itself called, and can one speak of a vocation for colleges and universities? Is a discussion of values a purely personal matter for the "free professional," a term used to designate the individualism of law and medical practice, or are values a communitarian issue?

To put the question another way: Are professorial obligations solely to the scholarly research norms of the individual's academic discipline, or are professorial obligations understood as intrinsically connected with community norms of teaching and service in colleges or universities? Education especially lacks sensitivity to the moral and institutional contexts of professions (Nord 1990). "Teachers as teachers—as professionals rather than technicians—are obligated to have the moral knowledge necessary to participate responsibly in public debate over educational policy" (p. 176).

Movement toward community

Teaching is essentially a communitarian act requiring students' cooperation (Adler 1990). Teachers mainly facilitate learning by collaborating with students as "cooperative artists" who aid the process of discovery by relying less on their own authority than on the authority inherent in their discipline. Thus, a kind of community is formed, furthered because the teacher is also a learner, a student along with the others (Adler 1990). Parker Palmer's perception is that knowing and learning are communal acts that create a common ground. The great teachers "stimulate active, not passive, learning and encourage students to be critical, creative thinkers, with the capacity to go on learning after their college days are over" (Boyer 1990, p. 24). Another takes up the same theme, indicating "a growing body of research suggesting that 'cooperative learning' models—where students teach each other or work together on joint projects—are clearly superior to competitive approaches" (Astin 1988, p. 7). The pursuit of truth is a personal journey for the scholar, but the truths one arrives at must be tested in the community. "An author becomes an authority when others recognize that what he or she has asserted on his or her own authority bears the ring of truth" (Schurr 1982, p. 319). (See the final section for discussion of the learning community.) At this point, we are concerned to establish a few of the ethical assumptions on which it is based. Before doing so, however, it is important to note that a communitarian pedagogy resonates with concerns about community in the larger American society (see, e.g., Bellah et al. 1985, 1991; "Responsive Communitarian Platform" 1991–92). "The Responsive Communitarian Platform" is clearly a response to the heightened individualism in U.S. society and the concomitant erosion of concern for the common good.

The erosion of the core curriculum and the rise of the elective system in the 1960s profoundly affected the learning community. Faculty were freed to teach their specialties; they had little reason to discuss common courses or goals in a core. To teach well, however, demands a sense of intellectual community, "a common commitment of scholars to approach learning as an integrative rather than a disaggregative enterprise. Just as good teaching stimulates students to learn from one another, so must it grow out of a collective commitment on the part of the faculty to be teachers and students to one another" (*Policy Perspectives* 1990a, p. 3). "It is a fluid process of observation and interpretation, of consensus and dissent, conducted within a far-flung community of seekers who agree upon certain assumptions, rules, procedures . . . " (Palmer 1990, p. 12).

A paradigmatic case: Blending teaching with research

Intrinsic to good teaching is a critical orientation to the body of knowledge studied. The educator does not simply pass on truth. Interpretation of text and an understanding of the method, context, or author's point of view demand a scholarship of research along with sensitivity to students' learning styles. The passing on of a tradition is closely allied to the critical spirit (Kimball 1986), thus blending with the research required of the skilled teacher.

A commitment to research entails a sharing of interpretation with peers. They alone will validate the research findings. How the sharing takes place could be intradepartmental, but a larger audience is necessary—the professional conference or journal. While the connection between teaching and research is logical, the problem, as presented in this section, is the strain that develops in competing obligations in the pressured environment of contemporary higher education. Though a correlation between teaching and research exists (Benditt 1990), for too many scholars and administrators (responsible for the reward system), the research has become an end in itself divorced from teaching.

Consequences of effective teaching that relies on research are the alteration of perceptions, that is, the shaping of character, and the increased ability to imagine possibilities. Because of the powers of professors to effect these changes, a balance must exist between the maintenance of neutrality on important topics and the expression of the teacher's own views to students. Without this balance, manipulation can easily take place. Because of the danger of manipulation, some consideration of the implicit curriculum is in order (see "Future Directions for the Learning Community").

Summary

The work in academic life, like any other kind of work, is laden with values and has a moral dimension that emerges from the ethical reflection characteristic of institutional self-scrutiny. Work contributes to personal identity, has a social meaning, and is best understood as a vocation or calling (Frankena 1976; John Paul II 1981). The scholar has considerable power "to define reality" for and exercise control over society in general and students in particular (Lebacqz 1985). Students are vulnerable before and unequal to the scholar; trust must characterize faculty-student relationships. Ultimately, however, professorial knowledge is not proprietary but communal, dedicated to the welfare of society through the transmission and extension of knowledge (Pellegrino 1989).

The role of the scholar can be conceived in four phases: teaching, discovery, application, and integration, each of which has its own ethical assumptions and problems. Often the competing needs of these roles cause conflicts for the scholar teacher/researcher. Perhaps most urgent are the competing needs of teaching and research. In responding to these problems, the scholar must balance individual with group realities and requirements. An important pedagogical concept to help achieve the balance is the learning community.

*How does one confront the array of novel, moral issues that
arise as the university becomes more and more entangled
with the outside world? I think that is something that presidents have to pay special attention to, because they are certainly the most important line of defense in trying to articulate the values of the institution . . .* (Derek Bok, cited in
McMillen 1990, p. A20).

*Such [transformational] leadership occurs when one or
more persons engage with others in such a way that leaders
and followers raise one another to higher levels of motivation and morality. Their purposes, which might have started
out as separate but related, as in the case of transactional
leadership, become fused. . . . But transforming leadership
ultimately becomes moral in that it raises the level of human
conduct and ethical aspiration of both the leader and the
led, and thus it has a transforming effect on both* (Burns
1978, p. 20).

Leadership in Higher Education
Leadership in higher education has been an area of intense
scrutiny over the past several years as the debate over the
quality of higher education continues and the demand for
assessment of outcomes grows. Attention in the media to
increased incidents of racism on campus, to alleged tuition
and price fixing, to calls for reform in athletics, to allegations
of admissions quotas, to falsification of scientific data, and
numerous other issues exerts increasing pressure on the leadership in higher education to deal decisively with the ethical
implications of these issues.

Leadership can be simply defined as "the process of per-
suasion or example by which an individual (or leadership
team) induces a group to pursue objectives held by the leader
or shared by the leader and his or her followers" (Gardner
1990, p. 1). Leadership becomes "ethical" by serving the common good, by being responsive and caring of constituents,
and by working within a framework of shared beliefs concerning standards of acceptable behavior. Effective leadership,
whether contrasted with management (Bennis and Nanus
1985; Burns 1978) or combined with management (Gardner
1990), is distinguished by vision that creates focus, by the ability to grasp the "big picture" and communicate meaning to
develop commitment, by engendering trust, and by fostering

the process of renewing values, goals, energy, and human possibilities.

The distinction between transactional and transformational leadership is that transactional leadership accepts and works within the structure as it is, while transformational leadership renews (Burns 1978). The transformational model of leadership includes the creation of a vision, the securing of others' commitment to it, and, finally, the institutionalization of change. Studies of leadership suggest that transformational leaders have integrity and deeply held values as well as substantial experience (Dill and Fullagar 1987). Transformational models focus on communicating values in a way that provides meaning and empowerment to followers. Comparing the culture and experience of business to the needs of higher education suggests a five-step process for developing transformational leadership: create readiness, overcome resistance, articulate a vision, generate commitment, and institutionalize implementation (Cameron and Ulrich 1986). This type of leadership has the most relevance to the ideal of ethical leadership with which this report is most concerned.

Leaders can serve as symbols of moral unity for their institutions (Gardner 1965). They help "lift people out of their petty preoccupations" and get them to confirm that their efforts remain directed toward "objectives worthy of their best efforts" (p. 12). Often this kind of leader seeks to extend important opportunities for making decisions toward others in the institution. The preference for shared governance itself reflects a democratically based ethical assumption that simultaneously values the contribution of the many and the executive efficiency of the one.

Two organizational models clearly related to leadership began to gain prominence in the 1980s and continue into the 1990s. The first, related to the emphasis on retrenchment and reallocation (reducing faculty and staff and discontinuing programs, for example), focuses on strategic planning; the second, borrowing from the study of business organizations as cultures (Peters and Waterman 1982), emphasizes the importance of institutional culture (Peterson and Mets 1987). These models, including an examination of the combination of the two perspectives (Chaffee 1984), move the task of leadership in the direction of a stronger presidential role. This role requires skill in organizing and guiding decisions in two areas: (1) making major decisions about the institutional mission in the face of external and internal opportunities and constraints, and (2) communicating a vision for institutional direction that empowers constituents to work toward shared goals. A classic study of leadership and organizational culture, which analyzes three distinctive liberal arts colleges (Antioch, Reed, and Swarthmore), suggests that a single leader—the president—can initiate change but that the institutionalization of that change depends upon the senior faculty's commitment; unusual, noteworthy, or seemingly unique visible practices; and, though less important, student subcultures that become, through their voluntary acceptance over a long period of time, believing supporters (Clark 1970).

Clearly, the moral and ethical vision of an institution of higher learning must be promulgated and protected by all its members. By virtue of their special position to articulate and disseminate that vision, however, college or university presidents must be particularly aware and committed to ethical concerns. These requirements are especially important in a learning community that, despite the often hierarchical distribution of power within which it must operate, seeks to recognize and value the multifarious voices of its diverse populations.

The presidential role
The president, as leader, is accountable for all that happens within the institution and assumes the obligation to provide ethical as well as academic leadership. Leadership is a moral act infused with a vision and a commitment to action. Every action taken—or not taken—conveys information about the values of the leadership. This axiom seems especially true with regard to the routine interactions centering around how presidents spend their time, the questions they ask, the reactions they make to critical incidents, and their decisions as to what or who gains rewards (Kouzes and Posner 1987). The president can set the moral tone of the institution by ensuring that ethical issues are raised and discussed (Perlman 1990). The president can help articulate the ethics of ethos inherent to the institution.

Reflections on the need for an ethical dimension to the college presidency include the suggestion that presidents have an "ethical imperative" to highlight the values and missions of their institutions (Enarson 1984) and the belief that the moral authority of the president and the moral dimension of the university are connected with moral direction set by the president (Laney 1984). In several essays, college presidents and others speak of the need for personal courage and for consistency in their own moral values and ethical stances (Fisher and Tack 1988; May 1990).

Institutions with a strong positive ethos are led by individuals who clearly articulate the values expected in a democratic community, including a respect for and a responsibility to others, a sense of justice and fairness, and the development of both character and intellect in a caring community. The leader must have a vision of the institution's ethical life and then be able to "make it live in the imagination of all the members of the community" (Grant 1988, p. 197).

The impact of leadership on an ethical issue is further illustrated in a description of two Catholic colleges with very similar mission statements whose contrasting levels of commitment and action by the leadership result in remarkably different institutional responses to the issue of achieving diversity (Zingg 1991). In one instance, the leadership, recognizing both a need to remain viable and a commitment to "building a pluralistic community," established strategies from recruitment to commencement to accomplish its goals. The administration involved faculty in planning, encouraged their support, and rewarded their efforts. In contrast, leadership at the other institution, although espousing the mission to underrepresented populations, chose to shelve an extensive task force report by faculty and administrators that proposed a master plan to address the challenge of diversity, citing it as an "inappropriate starting point." Despite similar demographic environments, representation by minorities at the first college reached 54 percent; at the second college, the number reached only 15 percent.

Shared governance

Although the role of leadership is attributed to the president within the college or university, the organizational characteristic of an institution of higher education that differentiates it from other organizations is the expectation that governance is a shared responsibility. Multiple sources of leadership, such as the faculty union or faculty senate leaders, need to be considered in the equation of power, and the characteristics of academic work and the various campus constituencies must also be factored in. Literature on structures of campus governance (Baldridge et al. 1977; Cohen and March 1974; Millet 1978; Mortimer and McConnell 1978) describes the distinctive organizational characteristics of academic institutions, including the often ambiguous and abstract goals, the desires of professional employees (faculty) and clients (students) for a part in decision making, and their special vulnerability to environmental factors.

Three models of academic governance have been described: *academic bureaucracy,* the *university collegium,* and the *university as political system,* with the leadership and management strategies implied by each (Baldridge et al. 1977). The academic bureaucracy model is seen as hierarchical, formal, and efficient, with the leader as the "hero" who possesses technical problem-solving skills. In colleges and universities, however, power is generally diffuse and goals often ambiguous; thus, the organization is vulnerable to environmental influence. The collegium, or "community of scholars," model is characterized by shared decision making, the professional authority of faculty members, and more humane education. The collegium manages by consensus, with its leaders considered "firsts among equals." This model often deals inadequately with conflict and the actual workings of the academic institution. The political model focuses on the processes of forming policy that encompass different interest groups with diverse viewpoints. These processes involve negotiation, bargaining, and external and internal influence and can offer useful insights to the bureaucracy and collegium models. Leaders in higher education would be more accurately described as "academic statesmen" whose critical skill is the ability to lead and facilitate the expertise of key administrators in the increasingly complex work of the university, especially in the processes of strategic decision making (Baldridge et al. 1977).

A study of patterns at 30 institutions representing different types of campuses results in four models of campus governance: the *dual-organizational model,* the *academic community model,* the *political model,* and the *organized anarchy model* (Millet 1978). The first three are equivalent to the models Baldridge et al. (1977) describe. The organized anarchy model was originally described earlier (Cohen and March 1974). Here, the leader is seen as managing the institution's activities by initiating or maintaining structures and processes through interpretation and reinforcement of institutional cul-

Multiple sources of leadership, such as the faculty union or faculty senate leaders, need to be considered in the equation of power. . . .

ture (that is, through the values and beliefs that organizational members share). The model has been criticized because it challenges widely held ideas about leadership.

This description emphasizes the president's leadership role and defines campuswide governance as an advisory process distinct from the president's management role (Millet 1978). Another approach discusses authority in academic governance, including faculty senates, collective bargaining, and faculty interaction, with administrators and students looking at distribution of authority and claims of legitimacy (Mortimer and McConnell 1978). It argues that those concerned with governance should look for ways to enhance joint involvement. A comprehensive description of theories of leadership in higher education suggests that leaders who use an integrated approach to governance that employs more than one organizational model might be more skillful in fulfilling the numerous and often conflicting expectations of their position (Bensimon, Neumann, and Birnbaum 1989). This "cybernetic" model (Birnbaum 1988) encourages more flexible responses to administrative tasks because the leader is aware of the multiple realities in the organization, of differing interests, perspectives, and values, and of the need to maintain a complex approach to administration. The usefulness of the integrated model in the promotion of an ethos of community resides in its emphasis on maintaining a creative balance among various organizational systems—bureaucratic, collegial, political, and symbolic. This model has the potential for uniting an increasingly diverse student body and motivating people with conflicting value systems to work together with a common purpose in an atmosphere that encourages collaboration and trust.

Institutional requirements versus faculty assumptions
Faculty expectations for involvement in decision making could represent the single greatest obstacle to directive leadership (Bensimon, Neumann, and Birnbaum 1989). Knowledge of academic governance and the facility to use multiple administrative responses seem to characterize more successful leaders. The classic hierarchial, directive leadership role college and university presidents have traditionally adopted appears to be antithetical to the creation of the ethos of community characterized by shared responsibility for governance. Faculty respond more positively to a leader who joins them

in dialogue about ways to shape and realize a vision rather than one who imposes a vision on them (Grant 1988).

Sociologists have analyzed the conflicts experienced by professionals who function within outside organizations (such as scientists in industry or doctors in hospitals). The professional is a master of a particular area of knowledge who is thereby granted a certain measure of autonomy of action. The institution to which these masters belong, however, often seeks to regulate and control their actions for purposes of efficiency and uniform quality. A conflict can erupt between masters, who might feel that they are best able to judge the value and execution of their work, and business managers or directors, who must coordinate the efforts of masters within broad organizational goals. The academic institution is an example of an organization made up of professionals. The scholar's sense of the value and importance of his or her research and teaching sometimes conflicts with the college's or university's need for measurement, accountability, and effectiveness. Contrasting characteristics of authority derived from an administrative position and those derived from professional knowledge affect an organization's structure and decision-making style (Etzioni 1964): Administrative authority resides in a power hierarchy, while professional knowledge is individual and nontransferable. The conflict created by these differences becomes more critical when it is necessary for financial reasons to justify the continuing existence of an area of study that for the individual professional is part of a personal identity system.

Practices of Leadership
Certain behaviors appear to energize individuals to uncommon commitment and to raise their level of ethical aspiration. The vision of a college or university (promulgated through the mission statement) presents a view of a realistic, attractive future that is better for the organization and the people in it. Encouraging collaboration and teamwork empowers others and enables them to act. Strategic planning is an approach that encourages integrative solutions to conflicting goals.

Creating the vision: The mission statement
Leaders articulate a vision and give direction to their institutions (Bennis and Nanus 1985; Fisher 1984). This articulated direction in higher education is based on and emerges from

the institution's mission statement. The mission statement
is to the college or university what the "capstone" moral philosophy course was to the 19th century curriculum: the syn-
thesis of all that the institution stands for in higher education
(Sloan 1980). The mission statement implies responsibility
to fulfill specific educational services for the constituency
identified to benefit from these services. The institution's distinctive qualities (such as resources) or particular commitments (such as meeting the needs of hearing-impaired individuals at Gallaudet College) are specified to attest to the
institution's capability to achieve its stated goals. Rethinking
and revising an institution's mission statement can afford a
critically important opportunity to discuss its essential values,
to discover what tensions might exist among the stated aspirations and those in practice. Such a process can be part of
strategic planning or of a process called a "values audit" (discussed in detail in the final section). Any process of this
nature requires widespread discussion among all constituents, a process of "community conversation" about priorities
in values.

The organizational saga and the telling of purposes and
proclamation of ideals that reflect the culture of the college
or university provide a historical and mythical context for a
mission statement (Clark 1970). Values are delineated in the
mission statement as a response to questions about purposes
or ends that transcend the segmented goals of courses or
majors. Shared values derived from the mission statement
communicate the meaning and significance of the organization. They foster strong feelings of personal effectiveness, promote high levels of loyalty to the institution, facilitate consensus about organizational goals, encourage ethical behavior,
and promote strong norms about working hard and caring
(Fisher, Tack, and Wheeler 1988). Leaders who are clear about
their values and whose behavior consistently reflects their
values make a significant difference in an organization.
"Before students can become concerned about and committed to equity and social justice, they must hear people talking
about and acting on these issues" (Barr and Upcraft 1990, pp.
86–87). Getting people committed to common goals is one
of the leader's most significant strategies. The process can be
encouraged by using the shared vision of the mission statement to foster collaboration, to build trusting relationships,
and to seek integrative solutions (Kouzes and Posner 1987).

Empowering others: Collaboration and trust

Collaboration as an approach to organization has gained new importance in higher education. Collaboration connotes a more intense relationship than cooperation and implies a relationship among equals pursuing a goal of mutual interest (Barr and Upcraft 1990). The idea of collaboration among the various constituents of institutions of higher education still faces strong natural barriers because of the lack of clear lines of communication in the organizational structure and because of the traditional individualistic nature of faculty. Major issues in both higher education and society, however, foster through necessity an increased reliance on collaborative efforts on the campuses.

Increasingly, college and university presidents are moving toward a leadership style emphasizing relational interaction involving collaboration and empowerment of everyone's potential. Peter Likins of Lehigh University speaks about the positive consequences of "managing less," of believing that "it's less critical to manage administrative details efficiently than it is to put our hearts into our missions, . . . to be a little more creative, a little less structured" (*Chronicle* 1990).

Trust is an essential element of organizational effectiveness. It could be the most basic value in an institution of higher education, because without it no sense of community is possible (Sanford 1980). The foundation of a trusting relationship is believing that the other person has integrity. The leader's behavior, meeting commitments and keeping promises, is more critical than any other person's in determining the level of trust that develops (Gardner 1990). Such a condition is necessary to promote the process of ethical reflection and the analysis of value judgments and assumptions used in the process of making decisions. "If participants are really to disagree or to analyze their own and each other's value judgments and assumptions, they have to trust one another" (Brown 1990, p. 185). The apparent lack of trustworthiness, however, is less likely to be related to the presence or absence of this character trait and more often attributable to a system of sometimes conflicting requirements for the roles of faculty and administrators.

The challenge for leadership is to search out innovative opportunities for collaboration among campus constituents and to support efforts that might have an effect on increasing the level of trust. James Laney, president of Emory University, asserts that the structure of the academic environment in the past supported personal ethics but that the current system, beset by the pressures of specialization and the lure of commercial success, must be reconstituted to foster moral discourse. He cites examples of means that exist to encourage dialogue about fundamental questions, including "final lecture" series, freshman seminars led by faculty and administration, interdepartmental courses on global issues, and university committees to address issues of a moral nature on which the academy should take a stand, such as divestment and sanctions against South Africa (Laney 1990).

Modeling the way: Integrative solutions

Searching for integrative solutions requires identifying what others want or need with clarity to satisfy the concerns of various constituents. It requires purposeful consultation and active listening to diverse opinions to encourage incorporation of differing views and sharing credit for solutions. Multiple agendas exist in which some will "win" and others will not. Ethical decision making will be enhanced by using moral imagination to consider all those who have a stake in the outcome (Smith and Reynolds 1990). If leaders espouse the importance of collaboration, then they need to structure opportunities for it to occur.

Strategic planning is one process that offers an opportunity for the faculty, administration, staff, and students to work collaboratively and constructively with conflicts in values. The beginning point is an understanding of the reality that different interests, perspectives, and values are represented and that an appreciation and respect for the fundamental intellectual values of the faculty professionals, for the values necessary for institutional effectiveness and overall integrity, and for the needs of staff and students are required.

"Strategic planning is . . . the process of developing and maintaining a strategic fit between the organization and its changing marketing opportunities" (Kotler and Murphy 1981, p. 471). The steps for the institution to follow include analysis of the external environment in the present and the probable future, determination of the institution's major resources, formulation of goals, formulation of a strategy based on cost-effectiveness, a necessary change in the organization's structure, and design of systems of information, planning, and control (Kotler and Murphy 1981). A study of 14 small private colleges dealing with financial decline presents two models of strategic management: the "adaptive" strategy model, which compares the organization to an organism that changes products and services to survive, and the "interpretive" strategy model, which sees the organization as a changing social contract that requires meaning, credibility, and commitment to survive (Chaffee 1984). The most resilient institutions are those that follow a combination of the two, with interpretive strategies guiding adaptive strategies (Chaffee 1984).

Strategic planning is participatory and highly tolerant of controversy. It is an active, outward process that focuses on keeping the institutional vision directed and oriented to the future. The process is synergistic, offering the possibility of discovering mediating values and integrative directions, which can then be creatively articulated in plans that can be specified and programs with assessable goals at each organizational level by the individual units in the institution. These plans and programs are then "owned" by those who determined them, based on the commitment of their energy and abilities and the resources allocated to them.

Ethical Decision Making

Situations of moral responsibility occur within the institutional roles of most, if not all, members of the campus community and are generally met by acting with others honestly, fairly, respectfully, and consistently. The increasing complexity of the kinds of issues presented in this report, however, with their multiple agendas and competing claims, creates a real dilemma in reaching the "right" decision. A brief review of three models of ethical decision making provides a framework for addressing, if not completely solving, these challenging issues.

Ethical decision making results from the act of reflection; to be effective, it must be a legitimate part of the everyday process of making decisions. Certain conditions prepare the environment for individuals to share their own value judgments, to consider opposing views, and to make the best decision possible: the empowerment of the process itself and the individuals participating in it, trust, inclusion of relevant stake holders, the flexibility of role and positional stance, and depth of inquiry, that is, asking the right questions (Brown 1990).

The process of rational and moral decision making to be used in conjunction with a set of "academic principles of responsibility" includes a proposed code of professional ethics for the academic community that involves personal, professional, systemic, public, and political principles (Reynolds and Smith 1990). Within the context of this code, the first step in making a moral decision is to define the concrete ethical issues, as not all issues have moral dimensions (instead, they could be primarily policy or legal issues, the responses to which can be more clearly spelled out). The second step is to review imaginatively the alternatives for resolving the issue. Conversation and discussion of the ethical issues at stake can generate a range of possibilities to be considered. The third step is to carefully consider each alternative in relation to the academic principles outlined as well as any other set of values. The fourth is to check the proposed solution against one's intuitive moral judgment, imagining oneself in the position of those individuals who will be affected by the decision. If intuitively the proposed solution matches the judgment from the third step, it is likely to be an informed ethical judgment. If not, a review of the second and third steps might be in order. Finally, one must act on one's best deliberative judgment. This type of ethical reflection also aids one to articulate clearly the ethical issues and the reasoning behind the decisions made.

In contrast with this model, another model of ethical reasoning describes the process of ethical decision making as having two distinct levels (Kitchener 1985). The first is intuitive, based on prior experience with ethical situations and similar to a "common-sense" response. (Intuition is also a part of the decision-making process outlined in the preceding paragraph.) When ethical issues become more complex, a second level of decision making could be necessary: the critical evaluative level involving, in a hierarchical fashion, ethical rules, ethical principles, and ethical theory (Kitchener 1985) (see Beauchamp and Childress 1979 or Kitchener 1985 for a discussion of the level of ethical theory).

Ethical rules include codes of conduct that apply to professional practice, similar to the academic principles formulated by Reynolds and Smith, which assist a responsible person in making an informed judgment. Ethical codes are generally developed by professional groups and organizations and follow a legal model, including both expected and prohibited behaviors. Codes can be used as teaching tools, as a method of socialization of new professionals to the values and standards of the specific profession, and as a guide for practical situations (Winston and Dagley 1985). In many cases, the codes become insufficient because of omissions or contradictory advice, such as that arising from responsibility both to the individual and to the employing institution. In these cases, ethical principles can provide a rationale for decision making.

Five ethical principles are particularly relevant for higher education: respecting autonomy, doing no harm, benefiting others, being just, and being faithful (Kitchener 1985; see also Beauchamp and Childress 1979):

1. *Respecting autonomy* means respect for the rights of individuals to make their own decisions, even if they seem to be mistaken, as long as the actions do not infringe on the welfare of others. This principle is especially relevant in situations involving advising, where individuals giving guidance need to be aware of the student's right to an independent decision. The principle of autonomy is also related to concerns for the rights of self-determination and the First Amendment, of increasing concern on college campuses. Autonomy is also tied to the concept of competence to make a decision. Competence is difficult to evaluate, but such an assessment could be necessary in working with college students, addressing such factors as age, mental status, alcoholism, or drug abuse (Kitchener 1985). The consequence of decisions, if critical or life threatening, must be weighed in considering competence.

2. *Doing no harm,* or nonmaleficence, refers to both psychological and physical harm and applies to policies and procedures of institutions as well as individual acts. Psychological harm is more difficult to define and document than physical abuse. Institutional policies and actions can affect an individual's feeling of self-worth or his or her opportunities for advancement.

3. *Benefiting others,* or beneficence, is the obligation to actively promote the health and welfare of others. This principle is an acknowledged goal of institutions of higher education and the professions that work within it. The intent to benefit, however, could conflict with the principle of doing no harm. If the potential for harm exists, "the ethical responsibility lies in finding the greatest balance of value over disvalue" (Kitchener 1985, p. 23).

---

4. *Being just* is to treat individuals fairly, especially when the rights of one individual or group are balanced against another. The paradox in this case is that justice does not mean that all persons should be treated the same. Special consideration might be necessary when some have not had equal access, such as in affirmative action programs or special accommodations for the physically disabled.
5. *Being faithful* is central to all helping professions, involving the core issues of trustworthiness, keeping promises, and being truthful and respectful. Faithfulness implies a special ethical obligation when two parties to an agreement are unequal in maturity and/or power, for example, between a student and faculty member or a student and the institution. The more powerful party has the obligation to go one step farther to ensure fairness and understanding with regard to the less powerful party. In an organization, the nurturing of trusting relationships is essential to the support of communication and the accomplishment of goals. The honest, straightforward presentation of information, the clarification of what is possible and what is not, and the following through on commitments together represent more than an ethical exercise: The assumption of these ethical criteria constitutes a highly effective way to lead an organization.

These five principles serve as ethically consistent, relevant guidelines—not absolutes—upon which ethical actions and decisions can be based. They would be overturned only by stronger ethical obligations, related to doing the least amount of avoidable harm.

A recent discussion of ethical issues and administrative politics asserts that, while this model lends itself to some administrative areas, it is not as helpful when political issues are involved (Upcraft and Poole 1991). Two potential conflicts are involved: individual values versus institutional values, and professional expectations for sound administration (management) versus moral leadership. A need exists to identify the moral dimension of a situation to understand clearly the *origin* of choices to be made and allow the political and moral aspects of a decision to inform each other (Upcraft and Poole 1991).

The conceptual framework places the individual and community on an axis that is intersected by another axis consisting of the distinguishing factors of management and leadership (Upcraft and Poole 1991). The first quadrant contains administrative skills like managing time, the second defines community relationships like recognized obligations and agreements, the third identifies personal values related to leadership, including courage, moderation, prudence, and responsibility, and the fourth contains community values as described by Boyer (1990): justice, openness, discipline, and caring. The value of this model is to identify the ethical implications of a decision to clarify the basis for compromise about conflicting issues. All three models provide useful frameworks for the act of reflection necessary to make an ethical decision.

Summary

The role of leadership of the college or university is attributed to the president, who has the obligation of ethical and academic responsibility. The organizational characteristic of higher education institutions that differentiates them from other types, however, is the expectation of shared governance. Successful leadership in higher education requires the ability to use more than one organizational model to respond to different situations and multiple realities. Collaborative efforts that encourage dialogue, an emphasis on the shared values of the mission statement, and the creation of an atmosphere of trust all contribute to integrative processes and solutions (in the process of strategic planning, for example).

Using the values expressed by the mission statement and ethical reflection as resources in decision making can positively affect the college's or university's response to problems presented by institutional functions and societal forces. Institutional functions like assessment, development of institutional funding, intercollegiate athletics, and admissions require firm direction to make the values of the mission statement operative in decision making. Societal forces, including demographic and enrollment trends and economic and social trends, bring both possible disruption and/or opportunity.

Models of ethical decision making help inform the practice of successful leadership in the face of ever-increasing complexities in higher education. The models have in common the process of defining the issues, making decisions by reviewing alternatives based on intuitive evaluation or on ethical rules and principles, deciding whether to carry out the action, and then implementing it using the best deliberative judgment.

*Students are important to the character of the institution
in that they are the material for much of its work. . . . They
come with personal inclinations and then informally relate
to one another in patterns that uphold their predispositions
or alter them. As a result . . . the student body becomes a
major force in defining the institution* (Clark 1970, p. 253).

Discovering an Ethical Dialectic

The culture of an institution of higher education reflects the
values and practices of its external environment, the institution's history and organizational structure, and the attitudes
of faculty, students, and administration. Ideally, the college
or university environment should be stimulating, challenging,
and rewarding, both intellectually and personally. At times,
however, it can seem inhospitable or even hostile, especially
for many of the more than 50 percent of students who leave
before graduating. Certainly, the environment can seem daunting even for those students who persevere to receive degrees.
This section focuses on students, whose rapidly increasing
diversity in preparation, behavior, age, values, and attitudes
poses a tremendous challenge to faculty and administration
to respond in a way that fosters learning and competence in
and out of the classroom. The relationship between students'
attitudes and values and the environment that supports or
challenges them stands as a complex and dynamic dialectic
of confirmation and rejection affecting the ethical positions
and choices of both the individual and the institution.

Bringing their attitudes and values with them, incoming
students interact with peers, faculty, and the institutional
authority structure to form new cultures and subcultures or
to reshape existing ones. Social structures and relationships
have powerful potential for enhancing ethical behavior
(Brown 1985; Gilligan 1982). The strength or distinctive
nature of the institutional ethos, the size and complexity of
the institution, and the leadership and influence of individuals
within the institution all affect the values and interests manifested in the campus climate and the overall effect of the college experience on students. These influences extend to students' involvement in curricular and extracurricular activities
and their relationships and interaction with faculty, other students, and administrators. The relationship between these
constituent elements of the ethical dialectic remains dynamic,
with each influencing and being influenced by the other. The

*Social
structures and
relationships
have powerful
potential for
enhancing
ethical
behavior.*

concluding portion of this section describes specific ethical dilemmas, including racism, sexism, substance abuse, and academic dishonesty, and reports on several studies that seek to address them from the perspective of community.

Theoretical Models for Assessing Students' Development

Research indicates that interaction between faculty and students in and out of the classroom is a primary factor in students' learning (Pascarella and Terenzini 1991). The ethical dimensions of these interactions are addressed in the concluding section; this section briefly surveys a range of developmental studies that provide theoretical support for that ethical inquiry. These theoretical investigations provide numerous examples of the ways in which even a superficial knowledge of the development theory of students can aid faculty in responding to students' increasingly diverse needs.

Today's educators must acquire a broader knowledge of the patterns of late adolescent development to positively influence individual students' growth and achievement and especially the subsequent development of a mature ethical self-awareness. Such knowledge is *essential* for the establishment and maintenance of a learning community environment. Theoretical models can help educators to assess differences in growth and development and in educational milieus. Models also help identify how the interaction of these conditions affects students' subsequent development, either positively or negatively. Extensive knowledge of formal theory, however, is not necessary for positively affecting students' development: It is just as important that educators and administrators have a broad knowledge of students' developmental characteristics to read cues from students and select strategies and tools to influence most effectively their growth and achievement. It *is* especially important to be knowledgeable about gender and cultural-ethnic differences in cognitive and psychosocial development. Research in these areas over the past 10 years has particular implications for college teaching, educational policies, and student affairs programs and services.

As a prelude to an ethical analysis of students' growth and achievement, this subsection presents a range of developmental theories using cognitive and psychosocial models with which to discover and assess basic issues of students' development. These theories help provide the data and analysis for which ethical assumptions and opinions must account. Major reviews of the research and theories on late adolescent and adult life span development constitute the knowledge base of students' development (Creamer and Associates 1990; Delworth, Hanson, and Associates 1981, 1989; Knefelkamp, Widick, and Parker 1978; Pascarella and Terenzini 1991; Rodgers 1980). While a complete description of each of these areas is beyond the scope of this report, a summary description of some of the most useful models and a summary of the more recent work to examine questions of difference resulting from gender, cultural-ethnic factors, and age provide an awareness of the wide variety of information available to educators.

Cognitive developmental models
Cognitive developmental theories attempt to describe the way in which individuals use thought processes or internal logic to make sense of their experiences. The use of these theories to promote learning derives from the fact that students at different stages learn best in different environments. These learning processes develop in response to one's interaction with the environment, and, in time, they gain in complexity. For students, cognitive development is affected by the balance of challenge and support they perceive in their environment and experience. Of particular relevance to this report is research that has included questions of knowing and valuing (Kitchener and King 1981; Perry 1968), moral development (Gilligan 1982; Kohlberg 1969, 1984), and faith development (Fowler 1981; Parks 1986).

Intellectual development. One scheme of intellectual development posits nine positions or stages, which are commonly grouped into four general categories: dualism, multiplicity, relativism, and commitment in relativism (Perry 1968; cf. Kitchener and King 1981). This work suggests that students' views of knowledge, which move from simplistic to complex through a series of developmental stages, determine both the perceptions of the teacher's role and the students' own roles as learners:

1. *Dualism.* Students answer intellectual questions based on external givens and view their task as one of finding and learning them. They have little capacity for handling conflicting points of view.

2. *Multiplicity.* Students acknowledge a plurality of points of view but have no established criteria to evaluate one against the other.
3. *Relativism.* Students recognize knowledge as relative and contextual and are able to think in complex and analytic ways. Knowledge is disconnected from "rightness," however, possibly causing confusion and feelings of alienation.
4. *Commitment in relativism.* Students accept a pluralistic view of knowledge and begin to act in terms of personal choice and commitment (Perry 1968).

Moral development. While this theory seeks to explain cognitive and ethical growth, another model focuses primarily on moral development. A theory of hierarchical stages has been developed to demonstrate how individuals reason about moral issues and decisions (Kohlberg 1969, 1971, 1972, 1975, 1981a, 1981b, 1984). The theory distinguishes three levels of moral development—*preconventional, conventional,* and *postconventional*—and attributes two stages of reasoning at each level (the sixth stage was later dropped because of an absence of empirical evidence to support it). At each stage, the primary concern is with the principle of justice. At the earlier stages, a sense of justice is based on the physical consequences of the violation of rules and the satisfaction of one's own needs. At the second level, the expectations of others are recognized, and behavior is guided by a need for approval. Respect for authority emerges as necessary to maintain the social order. At the final level, internalized moral principles guide actions on the basis of a social contract that acknowledges equality and mutual obligation.

Moral development and gender. Some of the most recent work in cognitive development theory has centered on questions of differences in cognitive structural development resulting from gender. The best-known theory in the area of gender difference is the discovery of a form of moral reasoning (Gilligan 1982) believed to be different from that described earlier (Kohlberg 1971). The latter study discusses "a different voice"—the "care voice"—and emphasizes the relationships between people and a concern for preventing psychological or physical harm. Kohlberg's theory, on the other hand, describes what can be called the "justice voice" in its emphasis on impartial analysis using rules and principles of fairness.

All men and women use both voices, but everyone prefers one voice over the other. Most, but not all, women (about 80 percent) prefer the care voice, and most, but not all, men (about 70 percent) prefer the justice voice (Gilligan 1982, 1986; Lyons 1983).

Perry's scheme was normed on male students. A seven-stage scheme for describing cognitive development in women is based on the belief that different themes exist in women's ways of understanding "self, voice, and mind" (Belenky et al. 1986). In this scheme, cognitive development begins in silence, the first stage, and moves in the second stage to received knowledge, listening to the voices of others for guidance. In the third and fourth stages, concerned with subjective knowledge, women begin the process of listening to an inner voice and to defining themselves by relying less on external expectations. Stages five and six, the stages of procedural knowledge, are those in which women learn to use reason in defining these positions and develop a preferred mode of learning, either separate knowing or connected knowing. The final stage, analogous to Perry's commitment in relativism, is that of constructed knowledge when the knower becomes part of all that is known.

The implications of these distinctions are important: It could be possible that most college teaching, educational policies, and student affairs programs favor one way of knowing over another. Care-voiced individuals, for example, seem to prefer collaborative discussion instead of competition and learning by listening to each other, rather than classes structured around dominance and subordination.

Faith development. A six-stage conceptual framework based on theological and psychological perspectives and the analysis of life stories can be used to interpret the development of faith, that is, the human necessity of composing meaning or a sense of the whole of life, the need to answer questions of how life really is (or ought to be) and what has ultimate value (Fowler 1981). It uses seven aspects of the capacity for faith at each of these stages to interpret the ongoing restructuring of faith in the direction of greater adequacy.

An elaboration of this work (Parks 1986) specifically considers faith in young adults by reexamining the transitional dynamics between the third and fourth stages: the shift from assumed, conventional faith to a critical, self-aware faith. This model relates cognitive development (using Perry's scheme) to the development of affect using the concept of dependency, the development of community or the network of belonging, and the development of forms of faith as reflected in the differing images of God. Higher education has a role to play:

> *If higher education is to initiate young adults into a self-conscious, realistic appraisal of the courage and costs of knowing, the institution must embody in its policies, practices, and prevailing attitudes a clear affirmation of the frustrations, fears, losses, confusions, and sometimes despair that can disorder the self on the journey toward truth* (Parks 1986, p. 151).

Psychosocial developmental models

Psychosocial models of development emphasize the importance of specific developmental tasks, issues, and events that occur throughout life and the individual's subsequent management of them. This type of development is significantly influenced by the interactions that take place between individuals and their environments, because the stimuli and challenges resulting from these interactions bring about change or growth.

Chickering's model. A major assumption of Chickering's model is that the central task of college students is the "establishment of identity" (1969). He describes the development of identity by postulating seven vectors of development that involve the student in a process of differentiating and integrating thought and behavior (cf. Erikson 1968). The term *vector* is used to indicate direction and magnitude (though direction is conceived of as spiral rather than linear). The seven vectors are achieving competence, managing emotions, developing autonomy, establishing identity, freeing interpersonal relationships, clarifying purposes, and developing integrity. The college environment is seen as a source of potential support and challenge for development, with the student mastering various issues. The model also suggests a sequence of development that can help with the design of programs that "fit" students' needs.

Gender issues. Much of the research in psychosocial development in the past has focused on the development of white males. More recent research focusing on the developmental processes of women has revealed certain differences in gender, and gender-related research on women has addressed the sources of feelings of mastery and pleasure (Baruch, Barnett, and Rivers 1983), the development of autonomy (Straub 1987; Straub and Rodgers 1986), and the development of identity (Josselson 1987). Research specific to men ranging from their twenties to forties has considered development in terms of socioeconomic class and urban and rural environments (Farrell and Rosenberg 1981).

The notable conclusion for educators based on the research on mastery and pleasure in women's lives is the variety of psychosocial patterns that resulted in their feelings of well-being (Baruch, Barnett, and Rivers 1983), principally in terms of achieving competent skill in a job that held high prestige. The main sources of pleasure were relationships with families, friends, or work colleagues. An implication of this research is that the development of instrumental and emotional autonomy (Chickering 1969) during the college years is especially important for women in later adulthood, because overidentification with spouse or children (defining self in terms of others) makes many women feel vulnerable, especially if either is lost.

The study of men (Farrell and Rosenberg 1981) argues for the need to develop interventions for men in the college years in the area of interpersonal relationships, especially to face the emotional crises of middle age, when work often becomes less important than interpersonal relationships. The college years are critical for developing capacities for free and intimate personal relationships (Chickering 1969), but for men, the formation of identity through assumptions and expressions of autonomy is society's dominant expectation, often leaving interpersonal issues unresolved. A possible antidote might be powerful messages of caring and belonging delivered during the college years and an institutional invitation to subscribe to an ethic of care (Kuh et al. 1991).

Boys and girls grow up in essentially different cultures, even in the same household, where women speak a language of connection and intimacy and men a language of status and independency (Tannen 1990). Boys tend to play in large, hierarchically structured groups in which high status is achieved competitively by taking charge. Girls play in small groups and have a best friend, and intimacy, cooperation, and being liked are important. As adults, men tend to engage in the world as an individual in a hierarchical social order, trying to achieve and maintain the upper hand, preserve independence, and avoid failure. Women, on the other hand, are part of a network of connections, seeking and giving confirmation and support, preserving intimacy, and avoiding isolation. The result of this knowledge should be to develop an awareness of these differences and learn how to "interpret" them rather than attempting to change either style.

Cultural and ethnic issues: African-Americans. Sociocultural influences are important considerations in understanding and assessing psychosocial development. Research on the psychosocial development of African-American students (Branch-Simpson 1985), for example, has identified some areas of overlap with Chickering's vectors. Special features of the psychosocial development of African-Americans include prominent religious and spiritual dimensions and the more pervasive influence of the family and extended family on African-American students. African-Americans pass through five developmental stages:

1. *Preencounter:* The stage during which an African-American identifies with the European-American worldview, including an emphasis on assimilation into the white world.
2. *Encounter:* The stage when an experience (or collection of experiences) forces an African-American to rethink his or her understanding of African-Americans' place in the world and a reinterpretation of initial views.
3. *Immersion-emersion:* The stage during which an individual first searches for a sense of self (immersion) in the world of blackness and begins to control his or her experiences (emersion) in that world.
4. *Internalization:* A later stage wherein several outcomes are possible—rejection of anything of value that is "not black," fixation at the third stage, or superficial internalization, a sense of satisfaction with self and interest in discussion and plans without concomitant action.
5. *Internalization-commitment:* The final stage wherein an individual intentionally commits to active reform in his or her community (Cross 1971, 1978, 1985). (This stage, however, might not actually be differentiated from the other stages [Helms 1990].)

Eight noncognitive variables are crucial to the success of African-American students: positive self-concept, realistic self-appraisal, management of racism, demonstrated community service, preference for long-range goals over the immediate gratification of needs, availability of a strong support system, successful leadership experience, and nontraditionally acquired knowledge (that is, knowledge gained outside formal educational settings, particularly in culturally relevant areas) (Sedlacek 1987).

Other ethnic and cultural populations. Ethnic groups and cultures other than white and African-American require developmental analyses that satisfactorily account for their special differences. Assessment of psychosocial development is extraordinarily complex, because it is multidimensional, interacts with intellectual processes that are also dynamic and changing, and depends on social and cultural contexts. The increased diversity of today's college student population points to a need to devise effective models and methods to ensure that individual differences will be recognized and addressed. Further development of measurement tools and methodologies will add to the knowledge of psychosocial development, but at present it is vitally important for all educators to be aware of the complexity and heterogeneity of the college student population and to recognize that individual subgroups cannot be viewed through the same perceptual lens.

Institutions need to develop ways to adapt to the student rather than the student to the institution.

Recent theoretical reviews related specifically to groups based on ethnicity, gender, age, and sexual orientation give some attention to programmatic implications for these different groups and the importance of enhancing interaction among peers (Moore 1990; Wright 1987).

Asian-Americans have certain cultural values that can affect their integration into the higher education community (Chew and Ogi 1987). Their comparatively strong sense of humility, restrained emotional expression, total devotion to family, and traditional view of women as commodities can result in misunderstandings. Their so-called status as a "favored minority" and stereotyping as math and science whizzes can also lead to feelings of isolation and resentment.

The Hispanic population has grown rapidly in recent years yet continues to lag in educational achievement. Many Hispanic students feel pressure and guilt over choosing a lifestyle that emphasizes assimilation and relinquishing their cultural identity over becoming part of the larger society while maintaining cultural identity (Quevedo-Garcia 1987). In fact, most Hispanic students identify with their family's country of origin and resent being grouped into the general category "Hispanic." Characteristically, most are very loyal to their families and communities. These choices produce major developmental challenges in the establishment of personal identity. Recognition of these characteristics has led to programs, such as orientation and special award ceremonies, that aim to draw parents and family into the students' life at school.

Native Americans represent a relatively small minority of college students. Typically, they delay entrance into college and experience difficulty in establishing relationships with members of non–Native American populations or identifying with aspects of the college community (LaCounte 1987). Institutions need to develop ways to adapt to the student rather than the student to the institution (Tierney 1991). "Instead of helping the student become integrated into the mainstream, we need to help our organizational participants—faculty, in particular—become oriented to their students" (p. 39).

International students are another population whose cultural and ethnic backgrounds influence their developmental experience. In addition to the usual developmental tasks, foreign students must also master those necessary to manage successfully in a new and different national environment. Perhaps most urgently, they must learn to function in an essentially alien environment in a language in which they are often only marginally proficient. Most problems associated with interpersonal relationships, social adjustments, and housing seem to be associated with difficulties in language (Lee, Abd-Ella, and Burks 1981). Peer support is especially helpful in overcoming these obstacles, and many institutions sponsor clubs and organizations that represent different national groups on campus.

Because of the stigmatization of homosexuality, research on gay and lesbian students and subsequent programmatic implications focus heavily on counseling and psychotherapeutic applications (see *Journal of Counseling and Development* 1989). Even this research is just beginning to be accepted and integrated into training for counselors (Iasenza 1989). For college students, whether of traditional age or not, wrestling with an identity that at best is not accepted and at worst is vilified can lead to deep confusion and panic, and these students might choose individual help from mental health professionals and hoped-for invisibility (Martin 1982). Increasingly, gay and lesbian students are openly forming organizations and demanding recognition. These students have reached higher levels in their formation of sexual identity and higher levels of self-acceptance.

Finally, adult learners (students over the age of 25)—once termed "nontraditional"—form the majority of part-time students, which overall is the fastest-growing population in higher education (Fischer 1991). Their developmental needs and tasks are considerably different from students of "traditional" age. A common characteristic of adult learners is their "transitional" status, comprised of three components—"moving in," "moving through," and "moving on" (Schlossberg, Lynch, and Chickering 1989). Adults move in by adopting a realistic sense of what to expect from the college experience. They move through by participating in experiences that help them integrate their educational with their personal lives. By graduation time, adult students move on by contemplating their next moves. The concept of "mattering" in this context means that students need to feel that they receive attention from staff, faculty, and peers who care about them and appreciate their adult status (Schlossberg, Lynch, and Chickering 1989). A sense of mattering to an institution enhances a student's involvement in the learning process, benefiting student and institution alike. Services like orientation, academic advising, and career counseling can be designed to address the special transitional needs of adults.

Addressing Values: Ethical Issues and Dilemmas
The increasingly complex and serious issues facing higher education argue for the pursuit of an ethical environment that consistently asserts the importance of human dignity, nourishes growth and achievement, and insists on respect in interpersonal communications and relations. The level of ethical functioning of faculty and administration has a direct effect on the level of ethical functioning that students demonstrate or attempt to achieve. Instances of racism, sexism, homophobia, substance abuse, academic dishonesty, and so on are especially likely to occur in environments that do not maintain

this respect for interpersonal communication. Across the country, institutions of higher education are amending codes of student conduct, responding to the pressure from various constituencies (legislators, the public, the courts, students and parents as consumers, for example) and to the increasing publicity about sexual abuse, alcohol abuse, crime on campus, and incidents of racial, gender-based, or religious intolerance. Although they are not reverting to the previous doctrine of in loco parentis, which the courts continue to reject, colleges and universities are moving away from the freedoms granted to students in the 1960s (Thomas 1991). The role of the higher education professional is to gain an understanding of the institutional context of these concerns through an ethical analysis that clarifies issues and highlights interconnectedness and social responsibility.

Racism

The issue of racism on the college campus is complicated by (and at times a reflection of) the nature of race relations in the United States and the expectation that institutions of higher education have a responsibility to promote the common good. The ethos provides a clear statement for students of what the institution values and maintains students' expectations that directly affect their development, attitudes, and responses. In certain instances, however, as in the case of racism on campus, a disjunction exists between formal policy and individual's or groups' perceptions and behaviors. Acceptance of the fact of institutional racism in the structure and process of the institution can be difficult for many members of the higher education community.

Five elements of organization influence universities' policies and practices, present examples of institutional racism, and suggest organizational changes that can have significant positive impact (Chesler and Crowfoot 1990, based on Terry 1981): *mission, culture, power, structure,* and *resources.* Some suggestions for institutional change include the generation of plural definitions of excellence—in research, teaching, and service (mission), advancement of scholarly epistemologies and curricula that embrace worldviews and knowledge of different cultures (culture), provisions for minorities for access to decision-making areas (power), the alteration of patterns of interaction to promote collaboration across existing groups and organizational boundaries (structure), and the provision of spaces that are comfortable and supportive for the gathering, collaborating, and celebrating of underrepresented groups (resources).

Comprehensive organizational change is required to combat racism, not just "image management" techniques, which typically result in sensitivity training sessions, multiple meetings and task forces, and the appointment of a special minority affairs person. The way to motivate permanent and significant change is to redefine self-interest to factor in the cost of institutional racism to the organization and the potential gains and rewards for the organization by overcoming it (Chesler and Crowfoot 1990).

Other work (Ascher 1990) suggests that institutions of higher education experience three stages, which are neither automatic nor irreversible, to improve equity. The first stage is a *reactive* response to pressure by minorities, with results similar to those of "image management" (that is, basically superficial changes to the existing power base for the purposes of rhetorical efficacy). In the second, *strategic* stage, planning is better coordinated, with greater emphasis on outreach and programs (particularly through the division of student affairs) to deal with mentoring, transition, and cultural celebration. Finally, in the *integrating* stage, institutional leaders promote the faculty's involvement and curricular change for all students, recognizing and valuing multiculturalism as a strength of the institution. A number of programs involve peer training and peer-initiated activities and interventions, examples of the second, strategic stage (Dalton 1991). These efforts create more opportunities for contact and interaction among different racial and ethnic groups on campus to counteract incidents of bias by promoting awareness and appreciation of racial and ethnic differences.

Freedom of expression
The issue of free speech has been hotly debated on many campuses. Some institutions have attempted to address so-called "hate speech" with carefully worded guidelines that do not impinge on constitutionally protected freedom of expression. As yet, public institutions whose statements have been tested in court have not met this stringent requirement. Some private institutions have prohibited bias-related speech and the appearance of outside speakers on campus based on interpretations of their mission statements.

A number of arguments have been advanced in favor of the free expression of ideas in a community of learning that are combined with clear and concise standards of behavior that foster the common good. One author, for example, calls for "an open community, a place where freedom of expression is uncompromisingly protected, and where civility is powerfully affirmed" (Boyer 1990, p. 17). Restrictive codes are not the answer; instead, institutions should "define high standards of civility and condemn, in the strongest possible terms, any violation of such standards" (p. 20). This issue is a very clear example of an instance where models of ethical decision making as described earlier provide a framework for making a difficult and probably compromise decision.

The campus climate for women

Women constitute over half the undergraduate student population and masters' degree recipients (Pearson, Shavlik, and Touchton 1989), yet their experiences on college campuses continue to be very different from men's. On the positive side, great progress has been made: Among *all* women (students and academic professionals), women now receive 34 percent of all Ph.D. degrees; they account for 38 percent of law school graduates, 30 percent of new medical school graduates, and 21 percent of new dental school graduates; over 300 women now serve as presidents of colleges and universities; and women make up 27 percent of all faculty. The number of courses in women's studies has risen to some 30,000, and increased attention has been paid to sexual harassment and date rape. On the negative side, discrepancies in salary still exist at every level; women hold only 12 percent of college and university presidencies (though the number has doubled in the last 15 years); 40 percent of undergraduate women report experiencing sexual harassment from male students, faculty, and staff; and the incidence of eating disorders is increasing (Leonard and Sigall 1989).

Negative outcomes for college women, such as the decrease from freshman to senior year in grades, career aspirations, and self-esteem (while these factors increase for men [Hall and Sandler 1982]), could be related to a climate that continues subtle discrimination against women. These subtle forms of discrimination ("micro-inequities"), those everyday behaviors that discount or ignore and have a detrimental effect on a woman's self-esteem, include sexist humor, sexual

harassment, interruptions in meetings or discussions, lack of
attentiveness and covert dismissal, confusion of social and
professional roles, and exaggerated focus on appearance
(Bogart 1989). The most disturbing evidence of a negative
climate, however, is the increasing number of acquaintance
rapes and sexual assaults and the continuing attitude that
blames the victim for provoking the encounter.

Sexism, like racism, is an institutional issue, and several
conditions are necessary for change to occur:

1. *Strong institutional leadership by the chief executive
   officer;*
2. *The presence on campus of one or more women who
   are catalysts for change;*
3. *Formal and informal networks of women to identify
   problems, set priorities, and develop new programs;*
4. *An overall strategic plan for institutional change* (Bogart
   1989, p. 388).

One hundred and fifty programs and policies have been identified that address specific needs of women and can be
adapted by other institutions (Bogart 1984). Some of them
include programs to encourage faculty to integrate new scholarship on and by women into traditional academic disciplines;
a variety of efforts to increase opportunities and role mod-
eling for women students in science, mathematics, engineering, business, and computer sciences; development of
leadership promoted through prizes, opportunities for men-
torship, and focused training; efforts to hire, grant tenure to,
and promote women; and the establishment of equitable
salaries. Other programs address issues in admissions, financial aid, continuing education, counseling, support services,
and sexual harassment. But basic institutional changes in both
structure and process are required to create an environment
where women will thrive.

One suggestion that promotes progress toward universal
egalitarianism and consists of a series of five ideas requires
no net financial cost to an institution (Rowe 1989). The first
is familiar and required as a precondition of the other four:
a basic commitment to equality and appropriate action in that
direction by the top administration. Specifically, leaders must
talk and write about diversity and publicly affirm its priority
in higher education. Leaders must hold staff accountable for
affirmative action and equal opportunity policies and

who?

empower them to recruit and mentor members of under-represented groups. The other four ideas include:

1. One-to-one recruitment, in which everyone takes the responsibility for bringing a woman or minority to campus as new staff or faculty member, speaker, or student;
2. The integration of responsibilities for mentoring into performance evaluations and the expectation of collaboration by senior and junior colleagues;
3. Networks of women administrators, faculty, staff, and students that are directed by senior administrators to identify problems, set priorities, and develop new programs, and are maintained as the personal responsibility of members;
4. Complaint systems that function formally and informally to deal with feelings, to give and receive data on a one-to-one basis, and to counsel and solve problems to help the complainant help himself or herself.

Alcohol use and abuse

Despite the continued presence on campus of drugs like marijuana and LSD and other hallucinogens (see, e.g., Dodge 1991), alcohol remains the drug of choice for college students. The majority of college students continue to consume and abuse alcohol on campus, despite alcohol awareness programs and, in many states, a legal drinking age of 21 (Gonzalez 1991). College students who drink excessively experience a variety of consequences, including hangovers, driving under the influence of alcohol, missing classes, fighting, and vandalism (Engs and Hanson 1988). Studies involving fraternity members indicate that approximately 90 percent drink at social gatherings (Kodman and Sturmak 1984) and that students living in Greek houses are more likely to abuse alcohol than those who do not (Globetti 1988). A recent study at the University of Florida comparing samples of students from 1983 to samples in 1988 shows little positive change in overall consumption of alcohol, knowledge about alcohol, and alcohol-related problems, despite an increase in educational programs (Gonzales 1991).

Alcohol abuse is an area where simple band-aid approaches have failed and where clarity in defining the issue is still lacking. External societal influences are contradictory, because a general lack of agreement exists in this country about what constitutes responsible alcohol-related behavior. The response of a class of students at the University of Vermont to statistics about alcohol use and abuse at their institution indicates their belief that an institutional effort with a perspective on values is required (Burrell 1990). Students suggest several steps (in addition to common educational programs and nonalcoholic alternatives):

1. *Integrate issues on alcoholism into projects and group discussions in required courses.*
2. *Ensure that faculty, staff, and administrators act as positive role models by treating the issue of alcohol abuse seriously and by eliminating [jokes] about students' drinking. . . .*
3. *Initiate intensive and comprehensive education for student personnel administrators that stresses the clarification of values, the enhancement of self-esteem, and the effects of alcohol abuse.*
4. *Implement harsher rules and regulations pertaining to alcohol use among students, including greater emphasis on class attendance, the attendance by freshmen in a short, for-credit course on alcohol information and its effects, and tough campus policies on alcohol use, especially in residence halls* (Burrell 1990, pp. 562–63).

These ideas, without explicitly stating so, imply the need for institutionally sanctioned and promoted opportunities for interconnectedness. To effect positive change, all members of the campus community must develop an understanding of the issue and accept the social responsibility for determining the specific drinking behaviors that are acceptable in that environment—an example of emphasizing shared values to build community responsibility.

Academic dishonesty

Concern about the level of students' academic integrity is increasing as reports about the frequency of cheating and the general acceptance of cheating increase. Informal polls indicate that as many as three-fourths of the student population on campuses today admit to some form of academic fraud (Gehring, Nuss, and Pavela 1986). Codes of academic integrity are assumed to be known or written and are not promulgated and emphasized as critically important to an academic environment. Also on the rise are the number of incidents of plagiarism perpetrated by public figures, from a U.S. Senator and presidential candidate to university presidents. Cases of the misrepresentation of scientific data have also increased.

Once again, an ethical dilemma needs to be approached from the perspective of increased communication and emphasis on shared values for the community. Clear definitions of the bounds of appropriate behavior for all members and groups in the community are required to achieve a common understanding of academic integrity. Specific suggestions for complete definitions and reviews of areas of possible disagreement are available (see, e.g., Fass 1990; Kibler et al. 1988), along with procedures for due process.

In addition to forging clear definitions of academic integrity and provisions for due process, a consideration of the environmental factors that affect the level of cheating on a particular campus should be considered. Some colleges and universities have a long-established history of honor codes, whereby students pledge not to cheat and to turn in fellow students when they suspect cheating. To a large degree because of the strength of the institution's culture, these codes work, except perhaps in instances like collaborative study, where definitions might be less clear. The large majority of institutions do not have these codes, however, and their students come from diverse backgrounds that might or might not have emphasized the importance of academic integrity. Students are under pressure to succeed to get a good job or to go to graduate or professional schools, and they have grown up in an era involving scandals and corruption by public figures, corporations, and private citizens.

Clarifying the relationship between cheating and grades and tests and changing aspects of the institutional climate will provide more meaningful options for sponsoring academic integrity than by simply blaming the "lapsed" moral standards of today's students. Students are more likely to cheat under certain conditions:

> *Students frequently report that cheating increases when students perceive tests or grading procedures to be unfair, when instructors are viewed as inattentive and inaccessible, when papers are not read and graded carefully, or when students perceive a very high level of cheating on the part of their classmates* (Fass 1990, p. 180).

Faculty can follow a number of suggestions for discouraging cheating, such as informing students about institutional policies regarding academic honesty and carefully explaining what they mean, avoiding the use of the same examinations over and over, and being present and attentive during examinations (Gehring, Nuss, and Pavela 1986). Whatever methods are used, a strong commitment to the highest standards is of paramount importance to an academic community. "Academic honesty can be learned and taught in an environment in which these issues are discussed openly and continuously" (Fass 1990, p. 182).

Summary
The community of men and women on today's campuses face increasingly complex problems that warrant ethical assessment. The ethical situation of the academic environment must be addressed on at least two basic and interrelated fronts: individual development and institutional climate. The dynamism inherent in the dialectic between these agents allows for subtle or overt change. Theoretical models for understanding students' development help to provide faculty and administrators with the data they need to make policy decisions to help direct students into the community of scholars and to make them feel welcome there. If this adjustment can be effected, students' learning can be enhanced and the mission of the institution realized.

The personal and social destructiveness of racism, sexism, and academic dishonesty, as evidenced by the endemic overuse of alcohol and other chemical substances and by the brutality of rape and other forms of sexual harassment, can be managed—if not entirely overcome—only by the successful inauguration of a community in which ethical and moral values are reasonably clear and consciously accepted by its constituency. The final section describes such a community and indicates how it can be established and maintained.

FUTURE DIRECTIONS FOR THE LEARNING COMMUNITY

When we destroy the community of scholars, dehumanized teaching and learning are the result. We will build community in these places only if we see that performance at the expense of community is no achievement at all (Palmer 1977, p. 25).

Introduction to the Learning Community

This report has suggested the growing support that the concept of the learning community has gained from scholars, many of whom now view it as essential to the processes and functions of higher education (Boyer 1987; Gabelnick et al. 1990; Trueblood 1991). Many professionals believe that the goals of administrators, scholars, and students are best accomplished in community.

Perhaps the increased interest in community on today's campuses is the result of the prevalence of such problems as alcoholism and other forms of substance abuse, sexism, racism, and a breakdown in traditional social values (Josephson Institute of Ethics 1990). In response to these problems, campus life is now seen as playing a pivotal role in higher education, one that cannot be divorced from the curriculum. The erosion of commitments to teaching and learning is clearly related to a decline in the quality of campus life (Carnegie Foundation 1990). In assessing the values and ethics of higher education, both campus and curriculum are integral to the moral life of colleges and universities. Community is an important way of bringing both dimensions of higher education together and providing a goal toward which administrators, faculty, staff, and students should work.

Many professionals believe that the goals of administrators, scholars, and students are best accomplished in community.

Foundations of Community: Strong Culture, Distinctive Ethos

Culture in higher education is understood as "the collective, mutually shaping patterns of norms, values, practices, beliefs, and assumptions that guide the behavior of individuals and groups in an institute of higher education and provide a frame of reference within which to interpret the meaning of events and actions on and off campus" (Kuh and Whitt 1988, pp. 12–13). A strong culture enhances the institution's mission. It is also a source of the institutional ethos, understood as "an underlying attitude that describes how faculty and students feel about themselves . . . comprised of the moral and aesthetic aspects of culture that reflect and set the tone, character,

and quality of institutional life" (Kuh and Whitt 1988, p. 47).
Culture and ethos are related: A strong culture enhances the
distinctiveness of the institutional ethos.

Culture and ethos provide the foundation for building community, reflecting both a capacity for relatedness and an epistemology that gives rise to a morality on which ethical reflection is brought to bear (Palmer 1987). The capacity for
relatedness between knower and known is possible only
within a spiritual realm; it is predicated upon love, which in
higher education means love of learning and love of learners
(Carnegie Foundation 1990).

The assessment of ethos, culture, and community reflects
a relatively recent approach to ethical analysis. The resolution
of cases through the use of normative theory was the method
used in applied and professional ethics for the last 15 to 20
years. This abstract, deductive approach to ethics, however,
rests upon a more fundamental view of the moral life. "This
view articulates a different conception of the role of 'theory'
in ethics. Here theory is not so much a body of general principles as a search for a connected view of things [that] develops in close relation to concrete cases and experience" (Sullivan 1990, p. 190; see also Palmer 1983). This ethics reflects
on custom and character—the ethos—and how they affect
the quality of human life.

The search for a connected view of things poses a question
about what values are found in the daily practices of institutional life. Practices reveal what a group believes. These
behavioral manifestations can then be held up to normative
scrutiny. For example, it is more productive to study the rate
at which African-American athletes graduate than to pass a
resolution in the university senate decrying racism on campus.
The empirical data on graduation rates clearly indicate institutional commitment to educating diverse student bodies
(which does not, of course, negate the need for academic
institutions to take stands on racism).

The setting for community
The stronger the culture, the greater the potential for a distinctive ethos characterized by honest self-awareness, empa-
thetic responsiveness, internal coherence, stable resiliency,
and autonomous distinctiveness (Kuh and Whitt 1988, citing
Heath 1981). A study of colleges with high faculty morale
points to these characteristics, indicating that such colleges

also have a strong sense of community (Rice and Austin 1988). They tend to be relatively small, religious-oriented liberal arts institutions with firm theological foundations. Each has a distinctive organizational culture, participatory leadership, organizational momentum, and faculty identification with the institution. Institutional practice is clearly in line with institutional preaching in these colleges. Values are integral to their identity: "They say what they do, in very clear terms—then, do what they say" (p. 53; see also Gaff 1989).

The difficult challenge presented by these success stories is that they are not representative of the variety of institutions in higher education in the United States. Are small, private, religious institutions the only ones that can practice what they preach? That is, are they the only schools that can exist as valuing, or learning, communities? What about secular public and private universities or comprehensive colleges with large faculties and student bodies? Are they capable of developing a strong culture, distinctive ethos, and sense of community? Do not their very size and competing interests perforce create a bureaucracy and a sense of impersonality that prevail over the capacity for relatedness that characterizes community? Does not the heterogeneity or diversity of faculty and student class, race, and ethnic and religious background challenge community building? These questions go to the heart of the matter in higher education; indeed, they even exceed the domain of academia and have relevance for understanding the nation at large. Campus concerns about diverse populations, a more inclusive canon, and the goals of higher education are microcosmic reflections of the larger issues of values in a heterogeneous society shaped by a plurality of values and opinions. Little doubt exists that size, heterogeneity, and pluralism pose challenges for the establishment of a learning community.

Small size characterizes those institutions that challenge the dominant values of the higher education system through their emphasis on the intellectual or learning community (Astin 1985: Kuh and Whitt 1988). Many of the schools in Rice and Austin's study (1988) are religious in origin. The religious tradition, in these cases the Christian one, impels institutions to search for meaning and transcendence, a move away from the search for survival, market share, and competitive edge. It is a challenge to the dominance of the academic community as well. Survival is not a trivial matter; however, it would appear that a distinctive mission and culture will do more to aid survival than a direct focus on survival, a thesis supported by management theory (Newton 1986; Peters and Waterman 1982; see also Frankl 1962 for a philosophical foundation to such theory).

The development of students' talents depends on the ability of the institution to involve the students in the various dimensions of classroom and campus. Institutional size is the only resource correlated to the development of this talent, and it is found in an inverse relationship (Astin 1985). This conclusion underscores the importance of the small liberal arts college as a setting for the learning community but also as a model for all institutions of higher education (Breneman 1990).

Difference and diversity among students
A case in point is the recent tendency on a number of campuses for racial and ethnic groups to separate themselves from the community at large. While group solidarity can provide individuals with a supportive environment, they often are exclusive and might reject the presence of outsiders. In such instances, the development of strong institutional cultures can be impaired, and no defining and encompassing ethos will grow.

Diversity, however, need not result in social isolationism. Berkeley now has a minority enrollment of more than 55 percent. No racial or ethic group dominates at the university, and, according to Troy Duster, director of the Institute for Social Change at Berkeley, this fragmentation "might lead to a social transformation—a society without a dominant group, capable of working in the multicultural world economy that is now forming" (DePalma 1991b, p. 7). Duster concludes that it is no longer a question of "how you can be like me" but "how we can understand each other."

While diversity is the great challenge to community in higher education, it also indicates new social realities that will confront students upon graduation. As a result, one cannot simply walk away from community because the student population is so diverse. It is a priority on the national agenda that cannot be ignored in higher education, one that must be pursued as a moral imperative despite the distortions presented in the popular press and the conservative right under the rubric of "political correctness" (D'Souza 1991; Genovese

1991; Schlesinger 1991; Woodward 1991a; see also *Change* 1992). The incorporation of a multicultural perspective has had a significant, though varied, effect on the curriculum, yet the canon is in place, demonstrating the important place diversity has assumed on campus (Levine and Cureton 1992).

The colleges in the study of high faculty morale (Rice and Austin 1988) combine particularity with openness. While vulnerable students receive support and a sense of belonging from membership in discrete affirming groups, these organizations have the potential to lead to tensions on campus and to set groups apart. A diverse student body challenges students both to affirm uniqueness and to reach out to one another (Carnegie Foundation 1990). The educational goal of building a just society is not in the far distance, however. It is a goal that requires careful construction of a curriculum that, on the one hand, opens students to other communities as well as their own yet, on the other hand, brings critical reflection to bear on all groups while enlivening the communities of which they are members (Clayton 1992).

A diverse student body can also influence programmatic and institutional policies to hire a similarly diverse faculty. The Department of Education recently indicated that standards of diversity can be appropriate to groups that accredit specialized academic programs, such as the Accrediting Council on Education in Journalism and Mass Communications, as opposed to groups that accredit institutions, such as the Middle States group (Jaschik 1991). Such a dual approach, however, can lead to conflict within an institution. Suppose the journalism and mass communications accrediting council imposed standards for diversity among faculty in an institution prohibited by its regional accrediting agency from imposing these standards. Not only would the viability of the communications program be in doubt: What message would be conveyed to students about academic policies toward minorities?

The affirmation of community is based on the belief that academe must emphasize specific shared values, maintain a common sense of direction and vision, and keep a passion that is founded on an epistemology of relatedness between knower and known. Often this affirmation seems in doubt. The quest for learning and knowledge has been replaced by concerns for "basic survival, market share, [and] competitive edge" (Rice and Austin 1988). Academic excellence often means a published faculty and national reputation—fame, size, and wealth (Astin 1985; Carnegie Foundation 1990; Pascarella and Terenzini 1991), not necessarily an expansion of the knowledge base (Schaefer 1990). Students are strangers and guests in all too many institutions, a pathetic reality (Cheney 1991; see also Wilson 1991). Community is central to the goals of higher education (Parks 1990). The loss of transcendent meaning began during the 18th century Enlightenment (Parks 1990; see also Sollod 1992).

The Learning Community versus the Academic Community

The commitment to powerful intercultural relations and an ethos of connectedness characteristic of the learning community appear at odds with some realities of the academic community. The academic community has tended to accord more privilege to research than to teaching, intellectual specialization than to broader forms of inquiry, and hierarchical rank than to more democratic relationships. The tendency in the academic community is for individuals to give allegiance to one's own discipline, not to colleagues from disciplines across the broader intellectual community. The *intellectual community* (Warch 1990), on the other hand, bears resemblance to the learning community.

The academic community and allegiance to one's discipline are not the only factors to consider in trying to understand that environment (Tierney 1988). The culture of the institution plays a central role in determining whether academic communities will dominate over the broader, intellectual community. Ascertaining the normative values of the institution therefore becomes imperative if the members are to examine their corporate identity and to make informed decisions about continuity and/or change in their institutional life. (Strategies for ascertaining these values are offered later.)

The tendency toward fragmentation and isolation in liberal arts colleges is challenged by the objectivism of the academic community and by advocating the relational epistemology of the learning community (Palmer 1983; Parr 1980; see also Association of American Colleges 1991). Advocating the learning community does not deny the value of research and publication, but they must be seen as goods internal to the practices of higher education (Burroughs 1990; Holly 1990; MacIntyre 1981), which benefit the community. If research and publication lead to tenure, economic security, and prestige, such external goods can erode the integrity of the practices themselves. External goods not only override students' learning, a primary internal good of higher education, but also raise questions about the quality of the research itself. If the research is not done primarily to expand the knowledge base but for extrinsic reasons, the research is vulnerable to manipulation arising from extrinsic motivation. Anxiety and reward could shape the interpretive framework guiding research inquiry.

Idealism and Intentionality in the Learning Community

Many see the development of community in higher education today as a response to a loss of direction and to disciplinary isolation (Carnegie Foundation 1990). It is viewed as a movement away from the pervasive individualism that exists in continuous tension with community in the United States (Bellah et al. 1985, 1991). Yet how can community be effective in a highly complex system representing not so much cultural pluralism that tends to value a range of opinion and experience as this strong strain of individualism that does not? In other words, how *practical* is this ideal of community?

The ideal community

Evidence of shared values among the various constituencies in higher education suggests the appropriateness of the community *ideal*. Yet it is certainly not the interdependence characteristic of family life; the intimacy and affectivity of blood ties are not the stuff of campus life. We should view instead collegiality in decision making, caring attitudes on the part of the faculty, and the profound influence of roommates and friends as principal interpersonal traits of community higher education. These relationships, at least in part, are what make higher education such an appealing calling for administrators and faculty; they are also a source of personal growth for students and of nostalgia for graduates.

Students and the student life staff comprehend how pervasive the learning experience is, especially for undergraduates. Faculty, when they distance themselves from their disciplines, know that learning takes place on campus in diverse ways, in unexpected situations, and through personal experience. Cognition and affection go hand in hand on both conscious and unconscious levels (Moffatt 1989). This learning is not only about ideas and how to think, but also in many situations contributes to the individual's personal development (Bok 1990). Keeping the campus honest is not only about ethics and values in the classroom; it is also about character and civic virtue: responsibility to and for others during the academic experience in preparation for life-long social responsibility.

The learning community, then, is an ideal-type, a utopian image that informs the search for meaning in higher education. Utopian images are not luxuries, available only during times of a balanced budget. Idealism challenges the law of the jungle in higher education: the struggle for survival in which college is pitted against college, demanding hard-nosed realism and bottom-line thinking as guidelines for educational policy. The image of the learning community seems to many to be a necessity, not a luxury.

Challenges to the ideal

Without a commitment to enhance those critical dimensions of a shared ethos, no discussion of the ethics of higher education will bear fruit. The challenge, many scholars insist, is to shift the prevailing forces on campus to create community based on a shared ethos. To effect this change, one must keep in mind the complexity of organizational structure in higher education in the United States. In public institutions of all types, the ideal of community meets resistance in the form of competing individual agendas (often to secure funding). Likewise, the image of community raises concerns over indoctrination and particularist religious values in an education system open to all by public mandate. These institutions are not founded by clearly defined communities that invest in the future of their own group. How does one develop a community around shared common values while still acknowledging some degree of affiliation to a particular group?

Certainly, a common commitment to getting good jobs through higher education is not a sufficient basis for such community. While smaller public and private institutions committed to the liberal arts tradition might have a better chance of developing a sense of community, large private universities are driven by the same centripetal forces as their public counterparts. And as students' age spread widens in all categories of institutions, community becomes even more difficult to achieve, because the adult learner is already part of other groupings (if not communities): work, family, church, and a variety of voluntary associations. Finally, community colleges, with their predominantly commuter population of all ages and interests, face similar challenges in building a sense of community. Thus, one must proceed with great caution in championing a cause that does not easily fit into the explicit or implicit missions of such a wide variety of institutions in a society that elevates the individual over the group, even if evidence exists of *some* homogeneity.

Freedom and intentionality

Local forms of community intent on civility and valuing both the intellectual life and the moral life should be constructed (Bellah et al. 1985; MacIntyre 1981). Community as a group is socially interdependent, participates in decision making, and shares practices of commitment that by nature are ethically good and transcendent in nature. *Intentionality* or freedom aptly describes both approaches.

The appellation "learning" associated with the concept of valuing community characterizes the intentionality that must be the foundation of life together in academe. Learning by its nature is characterized by freedom or intentionality; otherwise, it is memorization at best or indoctrination at worst. Learning communities are also understood as social forces that precipitate change; they "purposefully restructure the curriculum to link together courses or course work so that students find greater coherence in what they are learning as well as increased intellectual interaction with faculty and fellow students" (Gabelnick et al. 1990, p. 5). Inclusiveness, a balance between individual freedom and obligation to the group, the release of human possibilities, and an invitation to participatory leadership are contemporary values that also bring vitality to this learning community (Gardner 1989).

This discussion of community has paid attention to the strong presence in our society of individualism and to the complexity and size of institutionalized higher education. American individualism does not take society and, by extension, community as first-order realities (Bellah et al. 1985), a serious obstacle to building community. It would seem that heterogeneous race, ethnicity, and religion ironically mask a significant homogeneity of viewpoints: individualism above all else. One must wonder whether heterogeneity is more of a rationalization for avoiding community than a real philo-

Though they must be taken seriously, complexity and size are human constructs, not inevitable forces.

sophical problem. Though they must be taken seriously, complexity and size are human constructs, not inevitable forces. They are plastic, allowing for adaptation in view of needs and goals. It is individualism that is the most difficult to address because it is deeply rooted in our culture and directly challenges the possibilities of community as anything other than a derivative of individual utility (see especially Bellah et al. 1991, particularly chapter 5, for understanding this critical social issue).[1]

Moral ideals

The learning community is also a moral community (Mentkowski 1984), because "the quality of human relationships constitutes the moral dimension of human life" (Paris 1986, p. 146). Ethical reflection on and concerns about the moral dimension of the learning community presently abound, because the moral consensus in this community has been disrupted.

The development of learning communities—the "collegiate ideal" (Conrad 1984)—in higher education must, it is thought, be based on a transcendent premise (Wegener 1990). Inclusiveness and the commonweal can provide a moral framework (Dykstra 1990; Fleischauer 1984; Sherman 1984). The collegiate community is one that leads students beyond private interests and develops civic and social responsibility in the individual (Boyer 1987). These characteristics impel communities toward diversity in philosophy, gender, and ethnic groups within their own ranks. "Humans have the unique capacity to transcend every natural impulse and to envision and create new communities that are not regulated by natural needs and desires but by the goal of preserving and promoting our common humanity" (Paris 1986, p. 152). Internal transformation of the moral community, then, leads to collaboration with other communities. In this sense, the moral community is expansive, a characteristic essential to the learning community.

---

1. A new journal, *The Responsive Community,* published by the Center for Policy Research (2700 Virginia Avenue, N.W., Suite 1002, Washington, D.C. 20037) and edited by Dr. Amitai Etzioni, and the Institute for the Arts of Democracy, founded by Frances Moore Lappe and Paul DuBois (36 Eucalyptus Lane, Suite 100, San Rafael, California 94901, phone: 415-453-3333), are also important sources of information.

Strategies to Develop Community on
Campus and in the Classroom

The development and enhancement of community in higher education undoubtedly rests to a significant extent on the shoulders of student affairs personnel. Yet this responsibility is not one that they alone assume. Academic administrators and faculty also face the challenge of building community. The academic sector in reality is the keystone of any collegiate community. Why? The shape of a campus community is determined by the reasons for which the students and faculty are brought together—learning in all its diverse forms. Community is integral to these essential purposes of higher education and not a technique or palliative to diffuse tensions from racial or ethnic difference or political correctness. Given the fragmentation of the student body, with its diversity in ethnicity, size, age, part-time or full-time status, and commuter or residential status, an important means of forging unanimity in community is through the curriculum (Gabelnick et al. 1990). Today's curriculum bears the burden of establishing community in ways that the college as a whole did in the past).

The curriculum

The campus community is founded, in the first place, on learning. Learning, especially in the core curriculum, depends on a coherent curriculum that reinforces the connectedness of subject areas, thereby illuminating "larger, more integrative ends" (Carnegie Foundation 1990, p. 14), that is, a set of shared values. Connectedness through collaboration comes about when students from diverse majors are challenged to understand the subject from different points of view. Even though collaboration in specific courses can become problematic, it nevertheless remains fundamental to the core curriculum and underscores the communal nature of learning. Developing this core is itself a collaborative act on the part of faculty that communicates the truth of community to the students (Astin 1988).

The curriculum is an integral part of the college's larger culture, and every event on campus has implications for the curriculum (Gaff 1989). Thus, student affairs personnel have an important role to play. "They can help set high expectations, establish an intellectual tone in the student culture, and carry forward learning goals for students beyond formal course work" (p. 14).

Cultivating the love of learning

In addition to reinforcing the collaborative efforts of developing curriculum, it is essential to reinforce a context of mutual support or caring. Two forms of love—of learning itself and of the learner—are the binding forces for community (Palmer 1987). While the love of learners poses a more comprehensive challenge that embraces all dimensions of campus life, all members of the community are learners and all are challenged to this caring, both in the classroom and across the campus. The love of learners provides the supportive structure for any love of learning (Carnegie Foundation 1990), a love more directly related to the classroom or the laboratory (Palmer 1987). A campus community has six facets:

1. Freedom of expression in the open community;
2. Respect for the dignity of the person in the just community;
3. Acceptance of mutual obligations for the common good in the disciplined community;
4. Care for the well-being of each in the caring community;
5. Affirmation of tradition in the celebratory community;
6. Valuation of change in the community (Carnegie Foundation 1990).

These characteristics reflect personal as well as institutional values, and they are interdependent: The open community requires, at the same time, a just and disciplined community.

A well-developed concept of building community through a model of the just community has been tested in high schools, prisons, and college residence halls with some evidence to support its effectiveness (Higgens, Power, and Kohlberg 1984). The just community is "a group with an ongoing life (such as a student government) that governs itself through . . . participatory democracy" (Rodgers 1989, p. 137). Such groups seek a sense of community and rules of conduct through moral discussion groups and can be applied to the classroom as well (Galbraith and Jones 1976).

Instilling a love of learning depends, to a great extent, on the quality of the teaching faculty. "College, at its best, is a place where students, through creative teaching, are intellectually engaged" (Carnegie Foundation 1990, p. 12). If faculty do not stay close to their knitting, one cannot expect much from students. Two strategies to enhance community by instilling a love of learning focus on transforming the faculty reward structure (Barzun 1989; Carnegie Foundation 1991a; Paglia 1991; Wright 1991) and ensuring a classroom environment conducive to students' learning, understood as a communal act carried out by collaborative learning activities.

Administrative leadership

Central to any attempt to create a learning community is the role at all levels of administrative leadership. Leadership "means assuring that decision making at all levels will be based on high standards that are widely shared" (Carnegie Foundation 1990, p. 67). In fact, a look at the authority structure on a campus tells much about the possibilities for community on campus. The connection between leadership and morale (see, e.g., Rice and Austin 1988) has relevance for our interest in community. Certain modes of leadership, conducive to high morale, seem also to build community. Strong leadership is necessary for high morale, assuming that a variety of leadership styles (participatory *or* hierarchical, for example) are congenial with high morale (Rice and Austin 1988). The 10 colleges in the study of high faculty morale found "a leadership that was aggressively participatory" on both a personal and organizational level. Ironically, strong leadership—powerful presidents—yet "flat hierarchy" is possible. The presidents were servant leaders (Greenleaf 1977) who gave up power yet won the greatest of power by enhancing institutional effectiveness (DePree 1989; Samuels 1990). They freely shared information with the faculty, and relations with the board of trustees were open and unmediated by the administration.

The Values Audit: A Strategy to Enhance Community

In addition to inspiring the values implicit within the learning community, administrators (joined by others) must manage its practical implementation and evaluation. A principal strategy to accomplish these tasks is the *values audit,* a participatory process that can engender a sense of community, because it highlights the shared culture or system of values as well as conflicts in values (Smith 1984). Most often, values audits encourage the discovery of shared values through open dialogue and small-group discussion (although alternatives exist, as noted later). In short, a values audit is a critical investigation of the ethics of ethos within an institution of higher learning.

A study of the culture of higher education notes that "managerial control of culture and the extent to which cultural properties can be changed intentionally are more limited than some have suggested" (Kuh and Whitt 1988, p. 95). The subtlety of cultural influences and the subjectivity of individually constructed reality are key reasons for this lack of cultural flexibility (Kuh and Whitt 1988). Further, this inflexibility is reinforced not only by the enormous size of public higher education systems but also by legal constraints that prevent such systems' cultivating homogeneous student populations. Institutions of higher education, however, have some plasticity as a result of the diversity of the student body and its predictable turnover (Smith 1984). And the faculty are indeed diverse. Both groups can bring about change more easily than some anthropologists assume (Kuh and Whitt 1988). Administrative leadership can also have an impact on cultural change through the values it espouses and practices. Thus, individuals and institutions need to approach strategies for enhancing community with a sense of realism about and hope for change. A values audit is one way to test this reality and to effect change in the institution.

The assessment of a values audit piloted by the Society for Values in Higher Education notes that culture in colleges does not lend itself to manipulation. "The careful, intentional discussion of values can contribute to a greater self-consciousness about the culture of an institution and open the question of what elements should be strengthened," however (Smith 1985, p. 16). The conclusions are borne out by two values audits recently concluded at Manhattan College (1988 to 1990) and the College of Mount Saint Vincent (1989 to 1991), both located in the Bronx, New York.[2] The clarification of values or assumptions behind decision making do not eliminate divisiveness, but the significance of choices is

---

2. *The Values Audit Project of the Society for Values in Higher Education occurred in the early 1980s. It involved eight diverse institutions: three public universities, a public research university, two liberal arts colleges, and two church-related colleges (Berberet 1988; Gabelnick et al. 1990; Kirby et al. 1990; Smith n.d., 1984; "Values and Decision Making" 1986).*

clarified, alternatives are better defined, implications are more vivid, and, perhaps most important, there is "some sense of a common, public discourse amidst the diversity of interests and roles" (Smith 1985, p. 16). Perhaps most important, the values audit helps an institution to reach one of society's expectations regarding higher education: education in values. An explicit curriculum in such education in business or engineering is appropriate, but the institution itself must be inherently oriented toward values and ethically sensitive by practicing what it preaches.

Culture is holistic but has overlapping layers, making it difficult to understand. Yet an examination of culture helps in comprehending what is particular to an institution. Furthermore, a grasp of the assumptions that influence decision making is difficult but not impossible to attain (Kuh and Whitt 1988). Through such analysis, the dominant values and those of various subcultures are more easily revealed.

Comprehending culture calls for both understanding and appreciating the ethos, that is, "the affective dimensions of the organization, such as loyalty, commitment, and even love. . . . To preserve and enhance the unifying power of the ethos, social ties across constituent groups . . . must be maintained to sustain common belief systems" (Kuh and Whitt 1988, p. 98). Without a grasp of the ethos, it would be difficult to conduct a values audit, much less enhance community, as the latter would embody a distinctive ethos.

This report has emphasized that size and diversity in large public and private colleges and universities profoundly affect culture. In the establishment of a values audit for large institutions, the many subcultures among administration, faculty, students, and staff must be taken into account (Kuh and Whitt 1988, pp. 95–110). If one takes seriously Alasdair MacIntyre's belief that small intentional communities are the important elements in renewal, then the subcultures in higher education are the logical starting point for transferring the idea of the learning community from the smaller to the larger milieu. For faculty and students, it frequently means the department, discipline, or major. For administrators and staff, it might mean working with those individuals in the same area of responsibility. As indicated earlier, small liberal arts and comprehensive colleges serve as models for building community, because of size but also because of the centrality of a humanistic or religious vision.

Final Comments on the Learning Community

The learning community embraces a distinctive ethos, one that is laden with values and sustains the only fitting context for ethical analysis. Based on the curriculum, the learning community addresses many of the concerns in this report. For faculty who feel isolated by the limits of their discipline and miss the richness they knew so well in graduate school, the learning community enables them to reach out to other disciplines. At the same time, learning communities address the growing diversity among students in terms of age, race, ethnicity, religion, and marital and enrollment status. Most important, the learning community allows for a wide variety of application, not simply application in the small liberal arts college.

Within the learning community, the curriculum becomes the keystone in building community by addressing a host of problems at one time: coherence, civic responsibility, retention, active learning, and faculty development, all of which can be accomplished inexpensively and without institutional reorganization (Gabelnick et al. 1990). It also has the potential of creating community among faculty. Faculty organized in learning clusters at Babson College in Wellesley, Massachusetts, "agree on common themes, issues, problems, or historical periods to study in the cluster" (p. 24). Students have some common texts as well as speaking or writing assignments. A faculty seminar provides an opportunity to discuss individual and common syllabi. An ongoing faculty teaching seminar covers pedagogy and subject matter. In "federated learning communities," teachers who are Master Learners "report how demanding and illuminating it is . . . to be a learner in an undergraduate setting again and to reframe their own work in the context of different disciplines . . ." (p. 29).

Both curriculum (the disciplines that protect the value of knowledge) and the college as a whole (a time for growth toward self-fulfillment) are important (Mentkowski 1984). During 1967 on the campus of the University of Wisconsin at Madison, students had confronted Dow Chemical Company recruiters. "During the day, riots occurred, but the last whiffs of tear gas had all but disappeared when I emerged from my 'cell' later in the day. In some ways, the enforced discipline of a field of study was a source of stability, and specializing in one's discipline was a way to continue to see value in knowledge for its own sake" (p. 3). An assessment of students' development at Alverno College found students who achieved in the curriculum accelerated to a more balanced pattern of orientation to learning styles involving concrete experience/abstract conceptualizing, reflective observing/active experimenting (Mentkowski 1984). Alverno's success in developing a learning community among its students is in large measure the result of its focus on development of a comprehensive curriculum.

While learning communities are economical and can easily be geared to the needs of an institution, they need to be formally established if they are to be successful. Institutionalization requires flexibility and ongoing learning as well as planning and oversight. Academic innovation must be nourished, along with good feedback and support. Learning communities can support other educational reforms and stimulate faculty publication (Gabelnick et al. 1990). They can also support campuswide efforts to enhance community. Curricular reform that integrates into courses those qualities necessary for the open, just, disciplined, caring, or celebratory community (see Carnegie Foundation 1990) provides reinforcement for student life initiatives but also demonstrates to students the relevance of the curriculum.

Findings from outcome assessments indicate the value of the feeling of "belonging" on campus to retention. Learning communities go to the heart of the matter on campus—learning—and offer personal contact and group support: They let students know college is not a lonely experience. Some evidence also exists of higher achievement and improved intellectual development. Qualitative data on these communities show that students value, among other elements, the friendships and belonging, collaborative learning, greater intellectual energy and confidence, and the meaning of interdisciplinary study (Gabelnick et al. 1990).

Assessment of faculty indicates that learning communities are valued because they are rooted in the disciplines but reach out in a fairly safe structure. Faculty development in such projects avoids superficiality and involves pedagogy, not simply research. Individualism more easily gives way to collaboration.

In many ways, the learning community brings together key themes related to leadership, faculty, and students. Leadership is essential to colleges' and universities' increased sensitivity to values in higher education. The learning community symbolizes the delicate nature of that task. Faculty collaboration in this learning project is of the essence. Collegiality among administrators and faculty is clearly needed. These communities can bring out the best in faculty as well as resolve several of their tensions, especially the tension between research and teaching. Community gives direction to students and anchors their college experience in the intellectual life. Only such an approach will do justice to the complexity of ethical issues facing higher education.

REFERENCES

The Educational Resources Information Center (ERIC) Clearinghouse on Higher Education abstracts and indexes the current literature on higher education for inclusion in ERIC's data base and announcement in ERIC's monthly bibliographic journal, *Resources in Education* (RIE). Most of these publications are available through the ERIC Document Reproduction Service (EDRS). For publications cited in this bibliography that are available from EDRS, ordering number and price code are included. Readers who wish to order a publication should write to the ERIC Document Reproduction Service, 7420 Fullerton Rd., Suite 110, Springfield, VA 22153-2852. (Phone orders with VISA or MasterCard are taken at 800-443-ERIC or 703-440-1400.) When ordering, please specify the document (ED) number. Documents are available as noted in microfiche (MF) and paper copy (PC). If you have the price code ready when you call EDRS, an exact price can be quoted. The last page of the latest issue of *Resources in Education* also has the current cost, listed by code.

Adler, Mortimer J. 1990. "Beyond Indoctrination: The Quest for Genuine Learning." In *What Teachers Need to Know,* edited by David Dill and Associates. San Francisco: Jossey-Bass.

American Association of University Professors. 1984. *Policy Documents and Reports.* Washington, D.C.: Author.

———. 1987. "Statement on Professional Ethics." *Academe* 73(4): 49.

Ascher, Carolyn. 1990. "Recent Initiatives to Institutionalize Pluralism on Predominantly White Campuses." *Review* 2(1): 1–10.

Association of American Colleges. 1991. *Liberal Learning and the Arts and Sciences Major.* Vol. 1, *The Challenge of Connecting Learning.* Washington, D.C.: Author.

Association of American Medical Colleges. 1982. *The Maintenance of High Ethical Standards in the Conduct of Research.* Washington, D.C.: Author.

———. 1990. "Framework for Institutional Policies and Procedures to Deal with Misconduct in Research." Revised. Washington, D.C.: Author.

Astin, Alexander W. 1985. *Achieving Educational Excellence.* San Francisco: Jossey-Bass.

———. 1988. "The Implicit Curriculum." *Liberal Education* 74(1): 6–10.

———. 30 January 1991. "This Year's College Freshmen: Attitudes and Characteristics." *Chronicle of Higher Education:* A30+.

Audi, Robert. 1990. "The Ethics of Graduate Teaching." In *Morality, Responsibility, and the University: Studies in Academic Ethics,* edited by Steven M. Cahn. Philadelphia: Temple Univ. Press.

Baldridge, J. Victor, David V. Curtis, George P. Ecker, and Gary L. Riley. 1977. "Alternative Models of Governance in Higher Education." In *Governing Academic Organizations,* edited by Gary L. Riley and J. Victor Baldridge. Berkeley, Calif.: McCutchan.

Barr, Margaret, and Lee Upcraft. 1990. *The Future of Student Affairs.* San Francisco: Jossey-Bass.

Baruch, G., R. Barnett, and C. Rivers. 1983. *Lifeprints.* New York: Signet.

Barzun, Jacques. 1989. *The Culture We Deserve.* Middletown, Conn.: Wesleyan Univ. Press.

Beauchamp, Tom L., and James D. Childress. 1979. *Principles of Biomedical Ethics.* Oxford, Eng.: Oxford Univ. Press.

Belenky, Mary Field, Blythe McVicar Clinchy, Nancy Rule Goldberger, and Jill Mattuck Tarule. 1986. *Women's Ways of Knowing: The Development of Self, Voice, and Mind.* New York: Basic Books.

Bellah, Robert, Richard Madsen, William M. Sullivan, Ann Swidler, and Steven M. Tipton. 1985. *Habits of the Heart: Individualism and Commitment in American Life.* Berkeley: Univ. of California Press.

———. 1991. *The Good Society.* New York: Alfred A. Knopf.

Benditt, Theodore M. 1990. "The Research Demands of Teaching in Modern Higher Education." In *Morality, Responsibility, and the University: Studies in Academic Ethics,* edited by Steven M. Cahn. Philadelphia: Temple Univ. Press.

Bennis, Warren, and Burt Nanus. 1985. *Leaders: The Strategies for Taking Charge.* New York: Perennial Library.

Bensimon, Estela M., Anna Neumann, and Robert Birnbaum. 1989. *Making Sense of Administrative Leadership: The 'L' Word in Higher Education.* ASHE-ERIC Higher Education Report No. 1. Washington, D.C.: George Washington Univ., School of Education and Human Development. ED 316 074. 121 pp. MF-01; PC-05.

Berberet, William G. 1988. *Renewing the Liberal Arts Tradition.* Salem, Ore.: Willamette Univ.

Birnbaum, Robert. 1988. *How Colleges Work: The Cybernetics of Academic Organization and Leadership.* San Francisco: Jossey-Bass.

Bogart, Karen. 1984. *Toward Equity: An Action Manual for Women in Academe.* Project on the Status and Education of Women. Washington, D.C.: Association of American Colleges.

———. 1989. "Toward Equity in Academe: An Overview of Strategies for Action." In *Educating the Majority: Women Challenge Tradition in Higher Education,* edited by C.S. Pearson, D.L. Shavlik, and J.G. Touchton. New York: ACE/Macmillan.

Bok, Derek. 1990. *Universities and the Future of America.* Durham, N.C.: Duke Univ. Press.

Bok, Sissela. 1983. *Secrets: On the Ethics of Concealment and Revelation.* New York: Vintage Books.

Boyer, Ernest. 1987. *College: The Undergraduate Experience in America.* New York: Harper & Row.

———. 1990. *Scholarship Reconsidered: Priorities of the Professoriate.* Lawrenceville, N.J.: Carnegie Foundation for the Advancement of Teaching.

Branch-Simpson, G. 1985. "A Study of the Patterns in the Development of Black Students at The Ohio State University." Doctoral dissertation, Ohio State Univ.

Brandt, Edward N., Jr. 1987. "Research Administration in a Time of Change." *Journal of the Society of Research Administrators* 19(2): 5-8.

Breneman, David W. 1990. "Are We Losing Our Liberal Arts Colleges?" *AAHE Bulletin* 43(2): 3-6.

Broad, William J. 17 March 1991. "Cold-Fusion Claim Is Faulted on Ethics as Well as Science." *New York Times.*

Brown, Marvin T. 1990. *Working Ethics: Strategies for Decision Making and Organizational Responsibility.* San Francisco: Jossey-Bass.

Brown, Robert D. 1985. "Creating an Ethical Community." In *Applied Ethics in Student Services,* edited by H.J. Canon and R.D. Brown. New Directions for Higher Education No. 30. San Francisco: Jossey-Bass.

Buchholz, Rogene. 1989. *Fundamental Concepts and Problems in Business Ethics.* Englewood Cliffs, N.J.: Prentice-Hall.

Burns, James MacGregor. 1978. *Leadership.* New York: Harper & Row.

Burrell, Leon F. 1990. "College Students' Recommendations to Combat Abusive Drinking Habits." *Journal of College Student Development* 31(6): 562-63.

Burroughs, Catherine B. 1990. "Teaching and/or Scholarship." *Liberal Education* 76(5): 14-17.

Cahn, Steven M. 1986. *Saints and Scamps: Ethics in Academia.* Totowa, N.J.: Rowman & Littlefield.

Callahan, Daniel. 1982. "Should There Be an Academic Code of Ethics?" *Journal of Higher Education* 53(3): 335-44.

Camenisch, Paul F. 1983. *Grounding Professional Ethics in a Pluralistic Society.* New York: Haven Publications.

Cameron, Kim S., and David O. Ulrich. 1986. "Transformational Leadership in Colleges and Universities." In *Higher Education: Handbook of Theory and Research,* Vol. 2, edited by John C. Smart. New York: Agathon Press.

Caplan, Arthur L. 1980. "Evaluation and the Teaching of Ethics." In *Ethics Teaching in Higher Education,* edited by Daniel Callahan and Sissela Bok. New York: Plenum Press.

Carnegie Foundation for the Advancement of Teaching. 1990. *Campus Life: In Search of Community.* Lawrenceville, N.J.: Princeton Univ. Press.

―――. 1991a. "The Payoff for Publication Leaders." *Change* 23(2): 27-30.

―――. 1991b. "Research-Intensive vs. Teaching-Intensive Institutions." *Change* 23(3): 23-26.

Carter, Albert Howard. 1983. "The Teaching of Values in Colleges and Universities." In *Teaching Values and Ethics in College,* edited by Michael J. Collins. New Directions for Teaching and Learning

No. 13. San Francisco: Jossey-Bass.

Celis, William. 14 April 1991a. "All Involved Share Blame for Research Overcharges." *New York Times.*

———. 5 April 1991b. "U.S. Auditing Four Colleges for Expenses in Grants." *New York Times.*

Chaffee, Ellen E. 1984. "Successful Strategic Management in Small Private Colleges." *Journal of Higher Education* 55(2): 212–41.

Change. 1992. Special issue: "The Curriculum and Multiculturalism": 24(1).

Cheney, Lynne V. 1991. *Tyrannical Machines.* Washington, D.C.: National Endowment for the Humanities.

Chermside, Herbert B. 1985a. "Some Ethical Conflicts Affecting University Patent Administration." Part 1. *Journal of the Society of Research Administrators* 16(3): 23–34.

———. 1985b. "Some Ethical Conflicts Affecting University Patent Administration." Part 2. *Journal of the Society of Research Administrators* 16(4): 11–17.

Chesler, Mark A., and James E. Crowfoot. 1990. "Racism on Campus." In *Ethics and Higher Education,* edited by W.W. May. New York: ACE/Macmillan.

Chew, Charlene A., and Allen Y. Ogi. 1987. "Asian-American College Student Perspective." In *Responding to the Needs of Today's Minority Students,* edited by Donna J. Wright. New Directions for Student Services No. 38. San Francisco: Jossey-Bass.

Chickering, Arthur W. 1969. *Education and Identity.* San Francisco: Jossey-Bass.

Christensen, C. Roland, with Abby J. Hansen. 1981. *Teaching and the Case Method.* Boston: Harvard Business School Press.

Chronicle of Higher Education. 9 May 1990. "In an Era of Tight Budgets and Public Criticism, Colleges Must Rethink Their Goals and Priorities": B2.

Clark, Burton R. 1970. *The Distinctive College: Antioch, Reed, and Swarthmore.* Chicago: Aldine.

———. 1987a. *The Academic Life.* Lawrenceville, N.J.: Carnegie Foundation for the Advancement of Teaching.

———. 1987b. "Listening to the Professoriate." In *ASHE Reader on Faculty and Faculty Issues in Colleges and Universities,* 2d ed., edited by Martin J. Finkelstein. Lexington, Mass.: Ginn.

Clayton, Cornell W. 8 April 1992. "Politics and Liberal Education." *Chronicle of Higher Education:* B1+.

Cohen, Michael D., and James G. March. 1974. *Leadership and Ambiguity: The American College President.* Boston: Harvard Business School Press.

Committee on the Conduct of Science. 1989. *On Being a Scientist.* Washington, D.C.: National Academy of Sciences.

Conn, Steven. 1991. "Thoughts on National Service: An Open Letter to William F. Buckley, Jr." *Change* 23(3): 6–7+.

Conrad, Thomas R. 1984. " 'After Virtue' and Liberal Education." *Liberal Education* 70(2): 159–65.

Crawshaw, Bruce. 1985. "Contract Research, the University, and the Academic." *Higher Education* 14(6): 665–82.

Creamer, Donald G., and Associates, eds. 1990. *College Student Development: Theory and Practice for the 1990s.* Media Publication No. 49. Alexandria, Va.: American College Personnel Association.

Cremin, Lawrence A. 1980. *American Education: The National Experience, 1783–1876.* New York: Harper & Row.

Cross, William, Jr. 1971. "Discovering the Black Referent: The Psychology of Black Liberation." In *Beyond Black or White,* edited by J. Dixon and B. Foster. Boston: Little, Brown.

———. 1978. "Models of Psychological Nigrescence: A Review." *Journal of Black Psychology* 5: 13–31.

———. 1985. "Black Identity: Rediscovering the Distinction between Personal Identity and Reference Group Orientation." In *Beginnings: The Social and Affective Development of Black Children,* edited by M. Spencer, G. Brookins, and W. Allen. Hillsdale, N.J.: Lawrence Erlbaum.

Dalton, Jon C., ed. 1991. *Racism on Campus: Confronting Racial Bias through Peer Interventions.* New Directions for Student Services No. 56. San Francisco: Jossey-Bass.

Delworth, Ursula, Gary R. Hanson, and Associates, eds. 1981. *Student Services: A Handbook for the Profession.* San Francisco: Jossey-Bass.

———. 1989. *Student Services: A Handbook for the Profession.* 2d ed. San Francisco: Jossey-Bass.

DePalma, Anthony. 2 June 1991a. "Higher Education Feels the Heat." *New York Times.*

———. 18 May 1991b. "Separate Ethnic Worlds Grow on Campus." *New York Times.*

DePree, Max. 1989. *Leadership Is an Art.* New York: Dell.

Dill, David D., ed. 1982a. "Introduction [to Ethics and the Academic Profession]." *Journal of Higher Education* 53(3): 243–54.

———. 1982b. "The Structure of the Academic Profession: Toward a Definition of Ethical Issues." *Journal of Higher Education* 53(3): 255–67.

Dill, David D., and Patricia K. Fullagar. 1987. "Leadership and Administrative Style." In *Key Resources on Higher Education Governance, Management, and Leadership,* edited by M.W. Peterson and L.A. Mets. San Francisco: Jossey-Bass.

Dodge, Susan. 24 April 1991. "Drug Raids on Three Fraternities Force University of Virginia to Reexamine Its Traditions and Relations with Students." *Chronicle of Higher Education:* A33.

D'Souza, Dinesh. 1991. *Illiberal Education: The Politics of Race and Sex on Campus.* New York: Free Press.

Dykstra, Craig. 1990. "Communities of Conviction and the Liberal

Arts." *Council of the Societies for the Study of Religion Bulletin* 19(3): 61–66.

El-Khawas, Elaine. 1990. *Campus Trends, 1990.* Higher Education Panel Report No. 80. Washington, D.C.: American Council on Education. ED 322 846. 75 pp. MF–01; PC–03.

Enarson, Harold L. 1984. "The Ethical Imperative of the College Presidency." *Educational Record* 65(2): 24–26.

Engs, Ruth, and David Hanson. 1988. "University Students' Drinking Patterns and Problems: Examining the Effects of Raising the Purchase Age." *Public Health Reports* 103: 667–73.

Erikson, Erik. 1968. *Identity: Youth and Crisis.* New York: W.W. Norton.

Etzioni, Amitai. 1964. "Administrative and Professional Authority." In *Modern Organizations,* edited by Amitai Etzioni. Englewood Cliffs, N.J.: Prentice-Hall.

Farrell, Margaret P., and Steve D. Rosenberg. 1981. *Men at Midlife.* Dover, Mass.: Auburn House.

Fass, Richard A. 1990. "Cheating and Plagiarism." In *Ethics and Higher Education,* edited by William W. May. New York: ACE/Macmillan.

Finkelstein, Martin. 1983. "From Tutor to Specialized Scholar: Academic Professionalization in 18th and 19th Century America." *History of Higher Education Annual* 3: 99–121.

———. 1987. "Women and Minority Faculty." In *ASHE Reader on Faculty and Faculty Issues in Colleges and Universities,* 2d ed., edited by Martin J. Finkelstein. Lexington, Mass.: Ginn.

Fischer, Richard B. 1991. "Higher Education Confronts the Age Wave." *Educational Record* 72(5): 14–18.

Fisher, James L. 1984. *Power of the Presidency.* New York: ACE/Macmillan.

Fisher, James L., and Martha W. Tack. 1988. *Leaders on Leadership: The College Presidency.* New Directions for Higher Education No. 61. San Francisco: Jossey-Bass.

Fisher, James L., Martha W. Tack, and Karen J. Wheeler. 1988. *The Effective College President.* New York: ACE/Macmillan.

Fleischauer, John F. 1984. "Back to the Cave: Social Responsibility in Liberal Arts Education." *Liberal Education* 70(2): 113–19.

Fowler, James. 1981. *Stages of Faith: The Psychology of Human Development and the Quest for Meaning.* San Francisco: Harper & Row.

Frankena, William K. 1976. "The Philosophy of Vocation." *Thought* 51(203): 393–408.

Frankl, Viktor E. 1962. *Man's Search for Meaning: An Introduction to Logotherapy.* New York: Alfred A. Knopf.

Gabelnick, Faith, Jean MacGregor, Roberta S. Matthews, and Barbara Leigh Smith. 1990. *Learning Communities: Creating Connections among Students, Faculty, and Disciplines.* New Directions for Teaching and Learning No. 41. San Francisco: Jossey-Bass.

Gaff, Jerry G. 1989. "General Education at Decade's End." *Change*

21(4): 10–19.

Galbraith, R., and T. Jones. 1976. *Moral Reasoning: A Teaching Handbook for Adapting Kohlberg to the Classroom*. Minneapolis: Green-
haven Press.

Gardner, John W. 1965. "The Antileadership Vaccine." Annual report.
New York: Carnegie Corp.

———. Fall 1989. "Building Community." *Kettering Review:* 73–81.

———. 1990. *On Leadership*. New York: Free Press.

Gehring, Donald, Elizabeth M. Nuss, and Garry Pavela. 1986. *Issues
and Perspectives on Academic Integrity*. Columbus, Ohio: National
Association of Student Personnel Administrators.

Genovese, Eugene D. 15 April 1991. "Heresy, Yes—Sensitivity, No."
New Republic: 30–35.

Gilligan, Carol. 1982. *In a Different Voice: Psychological Theory and
Women's Development*. Cambridge, Mass.: Harvard Univ. Press.

———. 1986. "Reply by Carol Gilligan." *Signs: Journal of Women
in Culture and Society* 2: 324–33.

Giroux, Henry, and David Purpel, eds. 1983. *The Hidden Curriculum
and Moral Education*. Berkeley, Calif.: McCutchan.

Globetti, Gerald. 1988. "Student Residence Arrangements and Alcohol
Use and Abuse: A Research Note." *Journal of College Student Housing* 18(1): 28–33.

Goldman, Alan. 1980. *The Moral Foundations of Professional Ethics*.
Totowa, N.J.: Rowman & Littlefield.

Gonzalez, Gerardo M. 1991. "Effects of Awareness and Legal Drinking
Age on Alcohol Knowledge, Consumption, and Problems." *NASPA
Journal* 28(3): 243–50.

Grant, Gerald. 1988. *The World We Created at Hamilton High*. Cambridge, Mass.: Harvard Univ. Press.

Grassmuck, Karen. 12 September 1990. "Some Research Universities
Contemplate Sweeping Changes, Ranging from Management and
Tenure to Teaching Methods." *Chronicle of Higher Education*
37(2): A1+.

Greenleaf, Robert K. 1977. *Servant Leadership*. Ramsey, N.J.: Paulist
Press.

Gustafson, James M. 1991. "Ethics: An American Growth Industry."
Key Reporter 56(3): 1–5.

Hall, Roberta, and Bernice Sandler. 1982. *The Classroom Climate:
A Chilly One for Women?* Washington, D.C.: Association of American Colleges, Project on the Status and Education of Women. ED
215 628. 24 pp. MF–01; PC–01.

The Hastings Center. 1980. *Monographs on the Teaching of Ethics*.
Nos. 1–9. Pleasantville, N.Y.: Author.

———. 1984. *On the Uses of the Humanities: Vision and Application*.
Pleasantville, N.Y.: Author.

Heath, D.H. 1981. "A College's Ethos: A Neglected Key to Effectiveness and Survival." *Liberal Education* 67: 89–111.

Hechinger, Fred M. 9 December 1990. "Vandals with Ph.D.'s." *New York Times Book Review:* 28.

Helms, J. 1990. "An Overview of Black Racial Identity Theory." In *Black and White Racial Identity: Theory, Research, and Practice,* edited by J. Helms. New York: Greenwood.

Higgins, Ann, Clark Power, and Lawrence Kohlberg. 1984. "The Relationship of Moral Atmosphere to Judgments of Responsibility." In *Morality, Moral Behavior, and Moral Development,* edited by W. Kurtines and J. Gerwitz. New York: Wiley-Interscience.

Hilts, Philip J. 21 March 1991a. "Crucial Data Were Fabricated in Report Signed by Top Biologist." *New York Times.*

———. 22 March 1991b. "Hero in Exposing Science Hoax Paid Dearly." *New York Times.*

———. 28 March 1991c. "Panel Urges Independent Body to Set Ethical Standards in Science." *New York Times.*

Hirsch, Deborah. 1988. "Translating Research into Practice: The Impact of the Hidden Curriculum in Teaching Morals and Values." *Journal for Higher Education Management* 3(2): 45–51.

Holly, Carol. 1990. "Changes and Challenges." *Liberal Education* 76(5): 17–19.

Horowitz, Helen Lefkowitz. 1987. *Campus Life: Undergraduate Cultures from the End of the Eighteenth Century to the Present.* New York: Alfred A. Knopf.

Hunnicut, David M., Joe L. Davis, and Jennifer Fletcher. 1991. "Preventing Alcohol Abuse in the Greek System on a Commuter Campus: Prevention Contracts." *NASPA Journal* 28(2): 179–84.

Hutchins, Robert M. 1936. *The Higher Learning in America.* New Haven, Conn.: Yale Univ. Press.

Iasenza, Suzanne. 1989. "Some Challenges of Integrating Sexual Orientation into Counselor Training and Research." *Journal of Counseling and Development* 68(1): 73–76.

Institute of Medicine. 1989. *The Responsible Conduct of Research in the Health Sciences.* Washington, D.C.: Author.

Jaschik, Scott. 15 May 1991. "Some Accrediting Groups May Be Allowed to Use 'Diversity Standards.'" *Chronicle of Higher Education:* A1+.

John Paul II. 1981. *On Human Work.* Boston: St. Paul Editions.

Josephson Institute of Ethics. 1990. *The Ethics of American Youth: A Warning and a Call to Action.* Marina del Rey, Calif.: Author.

Josselson, Ruthellen. 1987. *Finding Herself: Pathways to Identity Development in Women.* San Francisco: Jossey-Bass.

Journal of Counseling and Development. 1989. Special issue: "Gay, Lesbian, and Bisexual Issues in Counseling": 68(1).

Kean, Thomas H. 1987. "Time to Deliver before We Forget the Promises We Made." *Change* 19(5): 10–11.

Kerr, Clark. 1991. "The New Race to Be Harvard or Berkeley or Stanford." *Change* 23(3): 8–15.

Kibler, William L., Elizabeth M. Nuss, Brent G. Paterson, and Gary
Pavela. 1988. *Academic Integrity and Student Development: Legal
Issues and Policy Perspectives.* Asheville, N.C.: College Adminis-
tration Publications.

Kimball, Bruce. 1986. *Orators and Philosophers: A History of the Idea
of Liberal Education.* New York: Teachers College Press.

Kirby, Donald, et al. 1990. *Ambitious Dreams: The Values Program
at LeMoyne College.* Kansas City, Mo.: Sheed & Ward.

Kitchener, Karen S. 1985. "Ethical Principles and Ethical Decisions
in Student Affairs." In *Applied Ethics in Student Services,* edited
by H. Canon and R. Brown. New Directions for Student Services
No. 30. San Francisco: Jossey-Bass.

Kitchener, Karen S., and Patricia M. King. 1981. "Reflective Judgment:
Concepts of Justification and Their Relationship to Age and Education." *Journal of Applied Developmental Psychology* 2: 89–116.

Knefelkamp, Lee, Carol Widick, and Clyde A. Parker. 1978. *Applying
New Developmental Findings.* San Francisco: Jossey-Bass.

Kodman, Frank, and M. Sturmak. 1984. "Drinking Patterns among
College Fraternities: A Report." *Journal of Alcohol and Drug Education* 29(3): 65–69.

Kohlberg, Lawrence. 1969. "Stage and Sequence: The Cognitive-
Developmental Approach to Socialization." In *Handbook of Social-
ization Theory and Research,* edited by D. Goslin. Chicago: Rand
McNally.

———. 1971. "Stages of Moral Development." In *Moral Education,*
edited by Clive Beck, Jerry B. Crittenden, and Edmund Sullivan.
Toronto: Univ. of Toronto Press.

———. 1972. "The Cognitive-Developmental Approach to Moral
Education." *Humanist* 32: 13–16.

———. 1975. "A Cognitive-Developmental Approach to Moral Education." *Phi Delta Kappan* 56: 670–77.

———. 1981a. *Essays on Moral Development.* Vol 1. *The Philosophy
of Moral Development: Moral Stages and the Idea of Justice.* New
York: Harper & Row.

———. 1981b. *The Meaning and Measurement of Moral Development.* Worcester, Mass.: Clark Univ. Press.

———. 1984. *Essays on Moral Development.* Vol 2. *The Psychology
of Moral Development: The Nature and Validity of Moral Stages.*
New York: Harper & Row.

Kolvenbach, Peter-Hans. 1990. "Jesuit Ministry and Higher Education." In *The Jesuits: Yearbook of the Society of Jesus.* Rome, Italy:
General Curia of the Society of Jesus.

Kotler, Philip, and Patrick E. Murphy. 1981. "Strategic Planning for
Higher Education." *Journal of Higher Education* 52(5): 470–89.

Kouzes, James M., and Barry Z. Posner. 1987. *The Leadership Challenge: How to Get Extraordinary Things Done in Organizations.*
San Francisco: Jossey-Bass.

Kuh, George, John Shuh, Elizabeth Whitt, and Associates. 1991. *Involving Colleges: Successful Approaches to Fostering Student Learning and Development outside the Classroom.* San Francisco: Jossey-Bass.

Kuh, George D., and Elizabeth J. Whitt. 1988. *The Invisible Tapestry: Culture in American Colleges and Universities.* ASHE-ERIC Higher Education Report No. 1. Washington, D.C.: Association for the Study of Higher Education. ED 299 934. 160 pp. MF–01; PC–07.

Kuhmerker, Lisa, Marcia Mentkowski, and V. Lois Erickson. 1980. *Evaluating Moral Development.* Schenectady: Character Research Press.

LaCounte, Deborah W. 1987. "American Indian Students in College." In *Responding to the Needs of Today's Minority Students,* edited by D.J. Wright. New Directions for Student Services No. 38. San Francisco: Jossey-Bass.

Laney, James T. 1984. "The Moral Authority of the College or University President." *Educational Record* 65(2): 17–19.

———. 1990. "Through Thick and Thin: Two Ways of Talking about the Academy and Moral Responsibility." In *Ethics and Higher Education,* edited by William W. May. New York: ACE/Macmillan.

LaPidus, Jules B., and Barbara Mishkin. 1990. "Values and Ethics in the Graduate Education of Scientists." In *Ethics and Higher Education,* edited by William W. May. New York: ACE/Macmillan.

Leary, Warren E. 25 March 1991. "On the Trail of Research Misconduct, 'Science Police' Take the Limelight." *New York Times.*

Lebacqz, Karen. 1985. *Professional Ethics: Power and Paradox.* Nashville: Abingdon.

Lee, Motoko Y., M. Abd-Ella, and L.A. Burks. 1981. *Needs of Foreign Students from Developing Nations at U.S. Colleges and Universities.* Washington, D.C.: National Association for Foreign Student Affairs. ED 203 776. 192 pp. MF–01; PC not available EDRS.

Lenn, Marjorie Peace, and D. Jeffrey Lenn. 1990. "Ethics and Educational Assessment: The Search for Quality and the Role of Accreditation in American Higher Education." In *Ethics and Higher Education,* edited by William W. May. New York: ACE/Macmillan.

Leonard, Mary M., and Brenda A. Sigall. 1989. "Empowering Women Student Leaders: A Leadership Development Model." In *Educating the Majority: Women Challenge Tradition in Higher Education,* edited by Carol S. Pearson, Donna L. Shavlik, and Judy G. Touchton. New York: ACE/Macmillan.

Levine, Arthur, and Jeanette Cureton. 1992. "The Quiet Revolution: Eleven Facts about Multiculturalism and the Curriculum." *Change* 24(1): 24–29.

Light, Donald. Winter 1974. "Introduction: The Structure of the Academic Profession." *Sociology of Education:* 2–28.

Lyons, N.P. 1983. "Two Perspectives: On Self, Relationships, and Morality." *Harvard Educational Review* 53: 125–45.

MacIntyre, Alasdair. 1981. *After Virtue.* Notre Dame, Ind.: Univ. of

Notre Dame Press.

McMillen, Liz. 14 November 1990. "An Interview with Derek Bok." *Chronicle of Higher Education:* A20.

Mangan, Katherine S. 29 July 1987. "Institutions and Scholars Face Ethical Dilemmas over Pursuit of Research with Commercial Value." *Chronicle of Higher Education:* 11–12.

Martin, A. 1982. "Some Issues in the Treatment of Gay and Lesbian Patients." *Psychotherapy: Theory, Research, and Practice* 19(3): 342–48.

Martin, Brian. 1989. "Fraud and Australian Academics." *Thought and Action* 5(2): 95–102.

May, William W., ed. 1990. *Ethics and Higher Education.* New York: ACE/Macmillan.

Meilaender, Gilbert. 1989. "The Ethics of Teaching Ethics: Introduction." In *The Annual: Society of Christian Ethics.* Washington, D.C.: Georgetown Univ. Press.

Mentkowski, Marcia. 1984. "The Institution as a Moral Agent." Paper read at an annual conference of the Association for Moral Education, November 9, Columbus, Ohio.

Millet, John D. 1978. *New Structures of Campus Power: Success and Failures of Emerging Forms of Institutional Governance.* San Francisco: Jossey-Bass.

Moffatt, Michael. 1989. *Coming of Age in New Jersey: College and American Culture.* New Brunswick, N.J.: Rutgers Univ. Press.

Moore, L., ed. 1990. *Evolving Theoretical Perspectives on Students.* New Directions for Student Services No. 51. San Francisco: Jossey-Bass.

Mortimer, Kenneth P., and T.R. McConnell. 1978. *Sharing Authority Effectively: Participation, Interaction, and Discretion.* San Francisco: Jossey-Bass.

Newton, Lisa H. 1986. "The Internal Morality of the Corporation." *Journal of Business Ethics* 5: 249–58.

Nickel, John W. 1990. "Do Professors Need Professional Ethics as Much as Doctors and Lawyers?" In *On Teaching,* Vol. 2, edited by Mary Ann Shea. Boulder: Univ. of Colorado.

Niebuhr, H. Richard. 1963. *The Responsible Self.* New York: Harper & Row.

Niebuhr, Reinhold. 1932. *Moral Man and Immoral Society.* New York: Charles Scribner's Sons.

Nord, Warren A. 1990. "Teaching and Morality: The Knowledge Most Worth Having." In *What Teachers Need to Know,* edited by David Dill and Associates. San Francisco: Jossey-Bass.

Pace, Charles R. 1979. *Measuring Outcomes of College: Fifty Years of Findings and Recommendations for the Future.* San Francisco: Jossey-Bass.

Paglia, Camille. 8 May 1991. "Academe Has to Recover Its Spiritual Roots." *Chronicle of Higher Education:* B1.

Palmer, Parker. 1977. *A Place Called Community.* Pamphlet 212. Wallingford, Pa.: Pendle Hill.

———. 1983. *To Know as We Are Known.* New York: Harper & Row.

———. 1987. "Community, Conflict, and Ways of Knowing." *Change* 19(5): 20–25.

———. 1990. "Good Teaching: A Matter of Living the Mystery." *Change* 22(1): 11–16.

Pamental, George L. 1988. *Ethics in the Business Curriculum.* Lanham, Md.: University Press of America.

Paris, Peter. 1986. "Expanding and Enhancing the Moral Communities: The Task of Christian Social Ethics." *Princeton Seminary Bulletin* 7(2): 145–56.

Parks, Sharon Daloz. 1986. *The Critical Years: The Young Adult's Search for Meaning, Faith, and Commitment.* New York: Harper & Row.

———. 1990. "Social Vision and Moral Courage: Mentoring a New Generation." *Cross Currents* 40(3): 350–67.

Parr, Susan Resneck. 1980. "The Teaching of Ethics in Undergraduate Nonethics Courses." In *Ethics Teaching in Higher Education,* edited by Daniel Callahan and Sissela Bok. New York: Plenum Press.

Pascarella, Ernest T., and Patrick T. Terenzini. 1991. *How College Affects Students.* San Francisco: Jossey-Bass.

Passmore, John. 1984. "Academic Ethics?" *Journal of Applied Philosophy* 1(1): 63–77.

Pearson, Carol S., Donna L. Shavlik, and Judith Touchton. 1989. *Educating the Majority: Women Challenge Tradition in Higher Education.* New York: ACE/Macmillan.

Pellegrino, Edmund D. 1989. "Character, Virtue, and Self-Interest in the Ethics of the Professions." *Update: Loma Linda Univ. Center for Christian Bioethics* 5(3): 1–6.

Perlman, Daniel H. 1990. "Ethical Challenges of the College and University Presidency." In *Ethics and Higher Education,* edited by William W. May. New York: ACE/Macmillan.

Perry, William. 1968. *Forms of Intellectual and Ethical Development in the College Years: A Scheme.* New York: Holt, Rinehart & Winston.

Peters, Thomas J., and Robert H. Waterman, Jr. 1982. *In Search of Excellence: Lessons from America's Best-Run Companies.* New York: Harper & Row.

Peterson, Marvin W., and Lisa A. Mets, eds. 1987. *Key Resources on Higher Education Governance, Management, and Leadership.* San Francisco: Jossey-Bass.

Policy Perspectives. 1989. Special issue: "The Business of the Business" 1(3).

———. 1990a. Special issue: "Back to Business" 3(1).

———. 1990b. Special issue: "Breaking the Mold" 2(2).

Potts, David B. 1981. "Curriculum and Enrollments: Some Thoughts on Assessing the Popularity of Antebellum Colleges." *History of Higher Education Annual* 1: 88–109.

Quevedo-Garcia, Ennio L. 1987. "Facilitating the Development of Hispanic College Students." In *Responding to the Needs of Today's Minority Students,* edited by D.J. Wright. New Directions for Student Services No. 38. San Francisco: Jossey-Bass.

"The Responsive Communitarian Platform: Rights and Responsibilities." 1991–92. *Responsive Community* 2(1): 4–20.

Reynolds, Charles, and David C. Smith. n.d. "Academic Leadership Styles, Institutional Cultures, and the Resources of Ethics." Washington, D.C.: Society for Values in Higher Education.

———. 1990. "Academic Principles of Responsibility." In *Ethics and Higher Education,* edited by William W. May. New York: ACE/Macmillan.

Rice, R. Eugene, and Ann E. Austin. 1988. "High Faculty Morale." *Change* 20(2): 51–58.

Rich, John M. 1984. *Professional Ethics in Education.* Springfield, Ill.: Charles C. Thomas.

Robertson, Emily, and Gerald Grant. 1982. "Teaching and Ethics: An Epilogue." *Journal of Higher Education* 53(3): 345–57.

Robinson, George M., and Janice Moulton. 1985. *Ethical Problems in Higher Education.* Englewood Cliffs, N.J.: Prentice-Hall.

Rodgers, R. 1980. "Theories Underlying Student Development." In *Student Development in Higher Education: Theories, Practices, and Future Directions,* edited by Don G. Creamer. Alexandria, Va.: American College Personnel Association.

———. 1989. "Student Development." In *Student Services: A Handbook for the Profession,* 2d ed., edited by Ursula Delworth, Gary R. Hanson, and Associates. San Francisco: Jossey-Bass.

———. 1990. "Recent Theories and Research Underlying Student Development." In *College Student Development: Theory and Practice for the 1990s,* edited by Don G. Creamer and Associates. Alexandria, Va.: American College Personnel Association.

Rosovsky, Henry. 1990. *The University: An Owner's Manual.* New York: W.W. Norton.

Rowe, Mary P. 1989. "What Actually Works: The One-to-One Approach." In *Educating the Majority: Women Challenge Tradition in Higher Education,* edited by C.S. Pearson, D.L. Shavlik, and J.G. Touchton. New York: ACE/Macmillan.

Ruscio, Kenneth P. 1986. "Values and the Structure of Decision Making: Finding the Connection in Higher Education." Paper presented at an annual meeting of the Association for the Study of Higher Education, February, San Antonio, Texas. ED 268 880. 29 pp. MF–01; PC–02.

Russ, Sandra, W. 1988. "The Professor." In *The Power of the Professional Person,* edited by Robert W. Clarke and Robert P. Lawry.

Lanham, Md.: University Press of America.

Samuels, Jay. 1990. "A Little Bit of Sugar Helps the Pill to Go Down." *Focus* 5(1): 1+.

Sanford, Nevitt. 1980. *Learning after College.* Orinda, Calif.: Montaigne.

Schaefer, William. 1990. *Education without Compromise.* San Francisco: Jossey-Bass.

Schlesinger, Arthur M., Jr. 1991. *The Disuniting of America: Reflections on a Multicultural Society.* Knoxville: Whittle Direct Books.

Schlossberg, Nancy K., Ann Q. Lynch, and Arthur W. Chickering. 1989. *Improving Higher Education Environments for Adults.* San Francisco: Jossey-Bass.

Schurr, George M. 1982. "Toward a Code of Ethics for Academics." *Journal of Higher Education* 53(3): 318-34.

Schuster, Jack H., and H. Bowen. 1987. "The Faculty at Risk." In *ASHE Reader on Faculty and Faculty Issues in Colleges and Universities,* 2d ed., edited by Martin J. Finkelstein. Lexington, Mass.: Ginn Press.

Sedlacek, William. 1987. "Black Students on White Campuses: 20 Years of Research." *Journal of College Student Personnel* 28: 484-95.

Shapiro, Harold T. 1990. "Reflections on the Future of University-Based Research." *Educational Record* 71(2): 48-50.

Sherman, Michael. 1984. "A Monologue of Counsel: Another Look at an Old Problem for the Humanities." *Liberal Education* 70(2): 102-11.

Shils, Edward. 1983. *The Academic Ethic.* Chicago: Univ. of Chicago Press.

Sigma Xi. 1984. *Honor in Science.* New Haven, Conn.: Author.

Sloan, Douglas. 1980. "The Teaching of Ethics in the American Undergraduate Curriculum, 1876-1976." In *Ethics Teaching in Higher Education,* edited by D. Callahan and S. Bok. New York: Plenum Press.

Smith, Arthur A. 1988. "Human Subjects and Informed Consent." *Research Management Review* 2(1): 1-4.

Smith, David C. n.d. "Values and Decision Making in Higher Education." Washington, D.C.: Society for Values in Higher Education.

———. 1984. "Program Improvement through Values Audits." In *Evaluation for Program Improvement,* edited by D. Deshler. New Directions for Continuing Education No. 24. San Francisco: Jossey-Bass.

———. 1985. "Values and Institutional Decision Making." *Academe* 71(6): 14-18.

Smith, David C., and Charles H. Reynolds. 1990. "Institutional Culture and Ethics." In *Ethics and Higher Education,* edited by William W. May. New York: ACE/Macmillan.

Smith, Page. 1990. *Killing the Spirit: Higher Education in America.*

New York: Viking Press.

Sollod, Robert N. 18 March 1992. "The Hollow Curriculum." *Chronicle of Higher Education:* A60.

Stewart, Donald M. June 1987. "The Ethics of Assessment." *Three Presentations from the National Conference on Assessment in Higher Education.* Washington, D.C.: American Association for Higher Education.

Straub, Cynthia. 1987. "Women's Development of Autonomy and Chickering's Theory." *Journal of College Student Personnel* 28: 198–204.

Straub, Cynthia, and Robert Rodgers. 1986. "An Exploration of Chickering's Theory and Women's Development." *Journal of College Student Personnel* 27: 216–24.

Streharsky, Charmaine J. 1988. "Scientific Misconduct: A Call for Institutional Principles." *Research Management Review* 2(2): 33–40.

Strike, Kenneth A. 1988. "The Ethics of Teaching." *Phi Delta Kappan* 70(2): 156–58.

Study Group on the Conditions of Excellence in American Higher Education. 1984. *Involvement in Learning: Realizing the Potential of American Higher Education.* Washington, D.C.: U.S. Dept. of Education, National Institute of Education.

Sullivan, William M. 1990. "Professional Ethics, Ethos, and the Integrity of the Professions." *Centennial Review* 34(2): 187–206.

Tannen, Deborah. 1990. *You Just Don't Understand: Women and Men in Conversation.* New York: Ballantine Books.

Terry, Robert. 1981. "The Negative Impact of White Values." In *The Impact of Racism,* edited by Bowser and Hunt. Beverly Hills, Calif.: Sage.

Thomas, Nancy L. 1991. "The New In Loco Parentis." *Change* 23(5): 33–39.

Tierney, William G. 1988. "Academic Work and Institutional Culture: An Analysis." Paper presented at an annual meeting of the Association for the Study of Higher Education, November, St. Louis, Missouri. ED 303 085. 24 pp. MF–01; PC–01.

————. 1991. "Native Voices in Academe: Strategies for Empowerment." *Change* 23(2): 36–39.

Tonnies, Ferdinand. 1963. *Community and Society,* translated and edited by Charles P. Loomis. New York: Harper Torchbooks.

Trueblood, D. Elton. Spring 1991. "The College in America." *Faculty Dialogue* No. 14: 7–20.

Upcraft, M. Lee, and Thomas G. Poole. 1991. "Ethical Issues and Administrative Politics." In *Managing the Political Dimension of Student Affairs,* edited by Paul L. Moor. New Directions for Student Services No. 55. San Francisco: Jossey-Bass.

"Values and Decision Making in Higher Education." 1986. Draft of Final Narrative Report. Lilly Endowment Grant No. 830094.

Waithe, Mary Ellen, and David T. Ozar. 1990. "The Ethics of Teaching

Ethics." *Hastings Center Report* 20(4): 17–21.

Warch, Richard. 1990. "Intellectual Community in Liberal Arts Colleges." Philadelphia: Pew Education Research Program.

Wegener, Charles. 1990. "Perfecting Intellectual Community." *Liberal Education* 76(5): 26–33.

Wheeler, David L. 20 September 1989. "Strict Guidelines on Potential Conflicts Proposed for Scientists Receiving Government Support." *Chronicle of Higher Education:* A1+.

———. 27 February 1991a. "Ethicist Urges Public Debate on Medical Therapies That Could Cause Genetic Changes in Offspring." *Chronicle of Higher Education:* A5+.

———. 15 May 1991b. "NIH Office that Investigates Scientists' Misconduct Is Target of Widespread Charges of Incompetence." *Chronicle of Higher Education:* A5+.

Wilcox, John R. 1989. "Professional Ethics." *New Catholic Encyclopedia.* Vol. 18. Washington, D.C.: Catholic Univ. of America.

Wilcox, John R., and Susan L. Ebbs. 1992. "Promoting an Ethical Climate on Campus: The Values Audit." *NASPA Journal* 29(4): 253–60.

Wilson, Everett K. 1982. "Power, Pretense, and Piggybacking: Some Ethical Issues in Teaching." *Journal of Higher Education* 53(3): 268–81.

Wilson, Robin. 9 January 1991. "Undergraduates at Large Universities Found to Be Increasingly Dissatisfied." *Chronicle of Higher Education:* A1+.

Winston, Roger B., Jr., and J.C. Dagley. 1985. "Ethical Standards Statements: Uses and Limitations." In *Applied Ethics in Student Services,* edited by Harry J. Canon and Robert D. Brown. New Directions for Student Services No. 30. San Francisco: Jossey-Bass.

Woodward, C. Vann. 15 & 22 July 1991a. "Equal but Separate." *New Republic:* 41–43.

———. 18 July 1991b. "Freedom and the Universities." *New York Review:* 32–37.

Wright, Barbara. 1991. "A Thousand Points of Flight." *Change* 23(2): 8–10.

Wright, Doris, ed. 1987. *Responding to the Needs of Today's Minority Students.* New Directions for Student Services No. 38. San Francisco: Jossey-Bass.

Wycliff, Don. 4 September 1990. "Concern Grows on Campus at Teaching's Loss of Status." *New York Times.*

Zingg, Paul J. 1991. "Missions Fulfilled and Forfeited: American Catholic Higher Education and the Challenges of Diversity." *Educational Record* 72(3): 39–44.

INDEX

A

AAUP
  ethics, 9
Academic
  bureaucracy, 31
  community, 68
  dishonesty, 59
  freedom, 10
  governance, models, 31
  integrity, 59, 60
  professions, 13
  role differentiation, 10
Accreditation
  specialized programs, 67
Adolescent development
  patterns, 44
  theories, 45
Adult learners, 53
African-Americans, 50
Alverno College, 79
American Association of University Professors
  code of ethics, 8
Antioch College, 29
Asian-Americans, 51
Athletic scandals, 5

B

Babson College, 78
Baltimore, David, 20
Beneficence, 39
Bok, Derek, 6
Boyer's topology, 11
Boyer, Ernest, 6

C

Campus community, 74
  curriculum, 73
Care-voiced individuals, 47
Center for Policy Research, 72
Cheating
  colleges and universities, 60
Chickering's model, 48
Codes of ethics, 7
  academic, 9
Cognitive development models, 45
Cognitive dissonance, 21
Collaboration and trust, 35
College of Mount Saint Vincent, 76

Ethical

    analysis, 54

    behavior, enhancement, 43

    decision making, 36, 37

    dialectic, 43

    dilemmas, 12, 60

    guidelines, 40

    leadership, 27, 28

    principles, 39

    principles, equal respect, 16

    principles, maximum benefit, 16

    rules, 38

Ethics

    colleges and universities, 5

    definition, 4

    educational institutions, 3

    of ethos, 3

Ethnic issues and dilemmas, 53

Ethos

    colleges and universities, 3

F

Faculty

    admission to, 14

    collective commitment, 24

    morale, 67

    plagiarism, 5

Faculty-student collaboration, 18

Faith development, 47

Faithfulness, 40

Federal audits

    research funds, 22

Florida, University of, 58

Foundations of community, 63

Fraternities, 58

Freedom of expression

    colleges and universities, 55

Freedom

    colleges and universities, 71

G

Gallaudet College, 34

Gay and lesbian students, 52, 53

Giamatti, A. Bartlett, 6

Graduate

    education, 15

    students, 15

Group solidarity, 66

H

Higher education
 code of ethics, 8
 culture, 63, 76
 leadership theories, 32
 service role, 12
Hispanics, 51
 personal identity, 52
Honor codes
 colleges and universities, 60

I

Ideal community, 69
Idealism
 learning community, 69
Identity establishment, 48
Imanishi-Kari, Thereza, 20
Individual scholarship, 22
Individualism, 71
Institute for Social Change, 66
Institute for the Arts of Democracy, 72
Institutional culture, 14, 15, 28
Institutional mission, 2
Institutional self-assessment, 1
Institutions of higher education
 culture, 43
 moral responsibility, 1
Intellectual development, 45
International students, 52
Involvement in Learning, 17

J

Justice, 40

L

Leadership practices
 colleges and universities, 33
Leadership
 colleges and universities, 5
 ethics, 27
 higher education, 27
 transactional, 28
 transformational, 28
Learning clusters, 5, 63, 68, 78
Learning community
 administrative leadership, 75
 institutionalization, 79
 moral values, 72

Shared governance
        colleges and universities, 30
Societal values, 8
Society for Values in Higher Education, 76
Stanford University
        overhead funds, 22
"Statement on Professional Ethics"
        AAUP, 8
Strategic planning
        colleges and universities, 36, 37
Student learning
        accountability, 18
Students
        assessing development, 44
        diversity, 66
        ethical analysis, 44
        psychosocial development, 44
Swarthmore College, 29

T
Teaching
        and research, 24
        characteristics, 12
Teacher-student relationship, 16
Tenure, 10

U
University as political system, 31
University collegium, 31
Utopian images, 70

V
Value audits, 2, 75
Value conflicts, 12
Vermont, University of, 59
Vocation
        colleges and universities, 23

W
Wisconsin, University of, 78
Women students
        discrimination, 56, 57
Women
        campus climate, 56
        cognitive development, 47
        mastery, 49
        pleasure, 49

ASHE-ERIC HIGHER EDUCATION REPORTS

Since 1983, the Association for the Study of Higher Education (ASHE) and the Educational Resources Information Center (ERIC) Clearinghouse on Higher Education, a sponsored project of the School of Education and Human Development at The George Washington University, have cosponsored the *ASHE-ERIC Higher Education Report* series. The 1992 series is the twenty-first overall and the fourth to be published by the School of Education and Human Development at the George Washington University.

Each monograph is the definitive analysis of a tough higher education problem, based on thorough research of pertinent literature and institutional experiences. Topics are identified by a national survey. Noted practitioners and scholars are then commissioned to write the reports, with experts providing critical reviews of each manuscript before publication.

Eight monographs (10 before 1985) in the ASHE-ERIC Higher Education Report series are published each year and are available on individual and subscription bases. Subscription to eight issues is $90.00 annually; $70 to members of AAHE, AIR, or AERA; and $60 to ASHE members. All foreign subscribers must include an additional $10 per series year for postage.

To order single copies of existing reports, use the order form on the last page of this book. Regular prices, and special rates available to members of AAHE, AIR, AERA and ASHE, are as follows:

Series	Regular	Members
1990 to 1992	$17.00	$12.75
1988 and 89	15.00	11.25
1985 to 87	10.00	7.50
1983 and 84	7.50	6.00
before 1983	6.50	5.00

Price includes book rate postage within the U.S. For foreign orders, please add $1.00 per book. Fast United Parcel Service available within the contiguous U.S. at $2.50 for each order under $50.00, and calculated at 5% of invoice total for orders $50.00 or above.

All orders under $45.00 must be prepaid. Make check payable to ASHE-ERIC. For Visa or MasterCard, include card number, expiration date and signature. A bulk discount of 10% is available on orders of 10 or more books, and 40% on orders of 25 or more books (not applicable on subscriptions).

Address order to
ASHE-ERIC Higher Education Reports
The George Washington University
1 Dupont Circle, Suite 630
Washington, DC 20036
Or phone (202) 296-2597
Write or call for a complete catalog.

1991 ASHE-ERIC Higher Education Reports

1. Active Learning: Creating Excitement in the Classroom
   Charles C. Bonwell and James A. Eison

2. Realizing Gender Equality in Higher Education: The Need to Integrate Work/Family Issues
   Nancy Hensel

3. Academic Advising for Student Success: A System of Shared Responsibility
   by Susan H. Frost

4. Cooperative Learning: Increasing College Faculty Instructional Productivity
   by David W. Johnson, Roger T. Johnson, and Karl A. Smith

5. High School–College Partnerships: Conceptual Models, Programs, and Issues
   by Arthur Richard Greenberg

6. Meeting the Mandate: Renewing the College and Departmental Curriculum
   by William Toombs and William Tierney

7. Faculty Collaboration: Enhancing the Quality of Scholarship and Teaching
   by Ann E. Austin and Roger G. Baldwin

8. Strategies and Consequences: Managing the Costs in Higher Education
   by John S. Waggaman

1990 ASHE-ERIC Higher Education Reports

1. The Campus Green: Fund Raising in Higher Education
   Barbara E. Brittingham and Thomas R. Pezzullo

2. The Emeritus Professor: Old Rank - New Meaning
   James E. Mauch, Jack W. Birch, and Jack Matthews

3. "High Risk" Students in Higher Education: Future Trends
   Dionne J. Jones and Betty Collier Watson

4. Budgeting for Higher Education at the State Level: Enigma, Paradox, and Ritual
   Daniel T. Layzell and Jan W. Lyddon

5. Proprietary Schools: Programs, Policies, and Prospects
   John B. Lee and Jamie P. Merisotis

6. College Choice: Understanding Student Enrollment Behavior
   Michael B. Paulsen

7. Pursuing Diversity: Recruiting College Minority Students
   Barbara Astone and Elsa Nuñez-Wormack

8. Social Consciousness and Career Awareness: Emerging Link
   in Higher Education
   John S. Swift, Jr.

1989 ASHE-ERIC Higher Education Reports

1. Making Sense of Administrative Leadership: The 'L' Word in
   Higher Education
   Estela M. Bensimon, Anna Neumann, and Robert Birnbaum

2. Affirmative Rhetoric, Negative Action: African-American and
   Hispanic Faculty at Predominantly White Universities
   Valora Washington and William Harvey

3. Postsecondary Developmental Programs: A Traditional Agenda
   with New Imperatives
   Louise M. Tomlinson

4. The Old College Try: Balancing Athletics and Academics in
   Higher Education
   John R. Thelin and Lawrence L. Wiseman

5. The Challenge of Diversity: Involvement or Alienation in the
   Academy?
   Daryl G. Smith

6. Student Goals for College and Courses: A Missing Link in Assessing and Improving Academic Achievement
   Joan S. Stark, Kathleen M. Shaw, and Malcolm A. Lowther

7. The Student as Commuter: Developing a Comprehensive Institutional Response
   Barbara Jacoby

8. Renewing Civic Capacity: Preparing College Students for Service
   and Citizenship
   Suzanne W. Morse

1988 ASHE-ERIC Higher Education Reports

1. The Invisible Tapestry: Culture in American Colleges and
   Universities
   George D. Kuh and Elizabeth J. Whitt

2. Critical Thinking: Theory, Research, Practice, and Possibilities
   Joanne Gainen Kurfiss

3. Developing Academic Programs: The Climate for Innovation
   Daniel T. Seymour

4. Peer Teaching: To Teach is To Learn Twice
   Neal A. Whitman

5. Higher Education and State Governments: Renewed Partnership,
   Cooperation, or Competition?
   Edward R. Hines

Values and Ethics in Higher Education

6. Entrepreneurship and Higher Education: Lessons for Colleges, Universities, and Industry
   James S. Fairweather

7. Planning for Microcomputers in Higher Education: Strategies for the Next Generation
   Reynolds Ferrante, John Hayman, Mary Susan Carlson, and Harry Phillips

8. The Challenge for Research in Higher Education: Harmonizing Excellence and Utility
   Alan W. Lindsay and Ruth T. Neumann

1987 ASHE-ERIC Higher Education Reports

1. Incentive Early Retirement Programs for Faculty: Innovative Responses to a Changing Environment
   Jay L. Chronister and Thomas R. Kepple, Jr.

2. Working Effectively with Trustees: Building Cooperative Campus Leadership
   Barbara E. Taylor

3. Formal Recognition of Employer-Sponsored Instruction: Conflict and Collegiality in Postsecondary Education
   Nancy S. Nash and Elizabeth M. Hawthorne

4. Learning Styles: Implications for Improving Educational Practices
   Charles S. Claxton and Patricia H. Murrell

5. Higher Education Leadership: Enhancing Skills through Professional Development Programs
   Sharon A. McDade

6. Higher Education and the Public Trust: Improving Stature in Colleges and Universities
   Richard L. Alfred and Julie Weissman

7. College Student Outcomes Assessment: A Talent Development Perspective
   Maryann Jacobi, Alexander Astin, and Frank Ayala, Jr.

8. Opportunity from Strength: Strategic Planning Clarified with Case Examples
   Robert G. Cope

1986 ASHE-ERIC Higher Education Reports

1. Post-tenure Faculty Evaluation: Threat or Opportunity?
   Christine M. Licata

2. Blue Ribbon Commissions and Higher Education: Changing Academe from the Outside
   Janet R. Johnson and Laurence R. Marcus

3. Responsive Professional Education: Balancing Outcomes and Opportunities
   Joan S. Stark, Malcolm A. Lowther, and Bonnie M.K. Hagerty

4. Increasing Students' Learning: A Faculty Guide to Reducing Stress among Students
   Neal A. Whitman, David C. Spendlove, and Claire H. Clark

5. Student Financial Aid and Women: Equity Dilemma?
   Mary Moran

6. The Master's Degree: Tradition, Diversity, Innovation
   Judith S. Glazer

7. The College, the Constitution, and the Consumer Student: Implications for Policy and Practice
   Robert M. Hendrickson and Annette Gibbs

8. Selecting College and University Personnel: The Quest and the Question
   Richard A. Kaplowitz

1985 ASHE-ERIC Higher Education Reports

1. Flexibility in Academic Staffing: Effective Policies and Practices
   Kenneth P. Mortimer, Marque Bagshaw, and Andrew T. Masland

2. Associations in Action: The Washington, D.C. Higher Education Community
   Harland G. Bloland

3. And on the Seventh Day: Faculty Consulting and Supplemental Income
   Carol M. Boyer and Darrell R. Lewis

4. Faculty Research Performance: Lessons from the Sciences and Social Sciences
   John W. Creswell

5. Academic Program Review: Institutional Approaches, Expectations, and Controversies
   Clifton F. Conrad and Richard F. Wilson

6. Students in Urban Settings: Achieving the Baccalaureate Degree
   Richard C. Richardson, Jr. and Louis W. Bender

7. Serving More Than Students: A Critical Need for College Student Personnel Services
   Peter H. Garland

8. Faculty Participation in Decision Making: Necessity or Luxury?
   Carol E. Floyd

1984 ASHE-ERIC Higher Education Reports

1. Adult Learning: State Policies and Institutional Practices
   K. Patricia Cross and Anne-Marie McCartan

2. Student Stress: Effects and Solutions
   Neal A. Whitman, David C. Spendlove, and Claire H. Clark

3. Part-time Faulty: Higher Education at a Crossroads
   Judith M. Gappa

4. Sex Discrimination Law in Higher Education: The Lessons of the Past Decade. ED 252 169.*
   J. Ralph Lindgren, Patti T. Ota, Perry A. Zirkel, and Nan Van Gieson

5. Faculty Freedoms and Institutional Accountability: Interactions and Conflicts
   Steven G. Olswang and Barbara A. Lee

6. The High Technology Connection: Academic/Industrial Cooperation for Economic Growth
   Lynn G. Johnson

7. Employee Educational Programs: Implications for Industry and Higher Education. ED 258 501.*
   Suzanne W. Morse

8. Academic Libraries: The Changing Knowledge Centers of Colleges and Universities
   Barbara B. Moran

9. Futures Research and the Strategic Planning Process: Implications for Higher Education
   James L. Morrison, William L. Renfro, and Wayne I. Boucher

10. Faculty Workload: Research, Theory, and Interpretation
    Harold E. Yuker

*Out-of-print. Available through EDRS. Call 1-800-443-ERIC.

ORDER FORM

Quantity   **Amount**

_____ Please begin my subscription to the 1992 *ASHE-ERIC Higher Education Reports* at $90.00, 33% off the cover price, starting with Report 1, 1992.   _____

_____ Please send a complete set of the 1991 *ASHE-ERIC Higher Education Reports* at $80.00, 41% off the cover price.   _____

_____ Outside the U.S., add $10.00 per series for postage.   _____

Individual reports are avilable at the following prices:

1990 and 1991, $17.00   1983 and 1984, $7.50
1988 and 1989, $15.00   1982 and back, $6.50
1985 to 1987, $10.00

Book rate postage within the U.S. is included. Outside U.S., please add $1.00 per book for postage. Fast U.P.S. shipping is available within the contiguous U.S. at $2.50 for each order under $50.00, and calculated at 5% of invoice total for orders $50.00 or above. All orders under $45.00 must be prepaid.

PLEASE SEND ME THE FOLLOWING REPORTS:

Quantity	Report No.	Year	Title	Amount

Subtotal:	
Foreign or UPS:	
Total Due:	

Please check one of the following:
☐ Check enclosed, payable to GWU–ERIC.
☐ Purchase order attached ($45.00 minimum).
☐ Charge my credit card indicated below:
    ☐ Visa   ☐ MasterCard

Expiration Date _____

Name _____

Title _____

Institution _____

Address _____

City _____ State _____ Zip _____

Phone _____

Signature _____ Date _____

SEND ALL ORDERS TO:
ASHE-ERIC Higher Education Reports
The George Washington University
One Dupont Circle, Suite 630
Washington, DC 20036-1183
Phone: (202) 296-2597